CHARLESTON
ALONE AMONG THE CITIES

LIMEHOUSE STREET. A portion of Limehouse Street, once on Charleston's waterfront, is seen here in a c. 1910 photograph during the landfill project that resulted in modern-day Murray Boulevard.

CHARLESTON

ALONE AMONG THE CITIES

SOUTH CAROLINA HISTORICAL SOCIETY

Copyright © 2000 by South Carolina Historical Society
ISBN 978-0-7385-0589-3

Published by Arcadia Publishing
Charleston, South Carolina

Printed in the United States of America

Library of Congress Catalog Card Number: 00-105403

For all general information contact Arcadia Publishing at:
Telephone 843-853-2070
Fax 843-853-0044
E-mail sales@arcadiapublishing.com
For customer service and orders:
Toll-Free 1-888-313-2665

Visit us on the Internet at www.arcadiapublishing.com

CONTENTS

ACKNOWLEDGMENTS

The editors wish to thank the following individuals for their assistance, advice, and expertise: Elise Pinckney, Robert Cuthbert, Betty and Francis Brenner, George Williams, Gene Waddell, and Ken Severens. We also would like to acknowledge the substantial role played by the staff of the South Carolina Historical Society, both past and present, in the development of the book. These individuals include Daisy Bigda, Heather Crosby, Susan Dick, Martha Fisher, Mary Giles, Steve Hoffius, Joe Holleman, Rhonda Hunter, Jacqueline McCall, Kathryn Meehan, Alexander Moore, Nancy Moreman, David Percy, Pete Rerig, Karen Stokes, Susan Welsch, Mark Wetherington, Peter Wilkerson, and Ashley Yandle. All of the images are from the collections of the South Carolina Historical Society.

VIEW LOOKING NORTH ON LEGARE STREET. Seen in the first third of the twentieth century, the mammoth homes in the foreground, numbers 8 and 10 Legare, were both constructed in the last decade before the Civil War. Farther up, on the same side of Legare, is the well-known "Pineapple Gates" House at Number 76.

INTRODUCTION

They tell me she is beautiful, my City
That she is colorful and quaint, alone
Among the cities . . . .

There is a natural tendency on the part of humans to compare one item, person, or place to another. Cities are often classed with one another; Toronto is, or was, a cleaned-up New York, Birmingham is the Pittsburgh of the South, Boston is the Athens of America, etc. For years writers have attempted to compare Charleston to some other town, usually Savannah, due to geography; New Orleans, owing to ethnic and architectural similarities, and even Venice, which some Charlestonians mutter after a deluge. A multitude of writers have spilled oceans of ink in the vain attempt to explain the splendid elegance and unworldly charm of the little city by the sea. Many have attempted to somehow compare Charleston to another place. Regrettably their effort is, in the main, wasted, for Charleston is above all unique, a singular creation, isolated for three centuries from all others: first by geography, later by politics, most recently by choice.

But I, I who have known
Her tenderness, her courage, and her pity,
Have felt her forces mould me, mind and bone,
Life after life, up from her first beginning.
How can I think of her in wood and stone!

Unfortunately, as Charleston has become the Mecca of tourists from all over the continent and the world that wish to see "the South," she has evolved into an architectural museum. The list of stylistic fashion is endless—Georgian, Adamesque, Regency, Greek Revival, Italianate, Norman Romanesque, Moorish Saracenic, Perpendicular Gothic, and on and on. Unlike many Northern cities, the buildings appear to have been placed where they are not to impress onlookers by their variety or aspiration to cultural refinement, but because they look beautiful there, suited to become a neighbor for several hundred years. While her buildings are jewels beyond measure, they are only the skeletal frame of what is a truly spiritual city.

The series of conflicts and disasters that have rocked the city over three centuries has forged its unique character. Five major fires, several fairly strong tremors, one earthquake of catastrophic dimensions, countless hurricanes, and two searing wars are the major landmarks in Charleston's history, a litany of disaster with which all residents, native and adopted, are familiar. Time

is measured from these events—for instance, present-day Charlestonians live in the era of Hugo, or "The Storm," the same as other generations who have marked time from "The Fire" or "The War" until the advent of the next disaster.

Though people "from away" now quip about the near mystical power of the conflict of 1861–1865, it has a real relevance to the discussion of any subject in Charleston. Nearly all of Charleston's white males from 15 to 50 were under arms at some point during the war; statewide, almost 80,000 men served. More than 20,000 never returned home, while those that did shouldered the burden of rebuilding a devastated, defeated land. Even in the 1890s a considerable portion of the city was still in ruins, and sustained economic recovery did not take place until World War II.

The earlier conflict, the American Revolution, was just as, if not more, divisive and a powerful factor in the city's development. Charleston was the scene of two major campaigns. In 1776 the British attempted to take the fortification on Sullivan's Island. This campaign failed, yet King George's men returned in 1780, captured the city, and accepted the surrender of a large American army. This grave defeat was the ebb of the Revolution. Some Americans did escape the British and began a partisan war against them. The leaders of the campaign are noteworthy figures in American history: Marion, Sumter, Pickens, and Lee. The savage fighting that took place in the South Carolina backcountry was truly a civil war, with brother assaulting brother, and families forever sundered. It was in the state's backcountry, at King's Mountain and Cowpens, that the tide of the war turned and Cornwallis began his fateful march to Yorktown.

The traffic and enslavement of humans is the other primal factor that has shaped the city. No one can walk the streets of Charleston without being confronted with the vestiges of the institution. Much of Charleston's built environment—homes, churches, walls, and gates—were the product of enslaved artisans. South Carolina was the only colony to have African slaves from the outset; its laws and culture developed accordingly. The influence of these slaves was beyond ubiquitous, it was overwhelming. Agriculture, foodways, building methods, music, language, and countless other aspects of Lowcountry culture all bear the imprint of African influences.

This character is what truly makes her unique. Though the city is now a showplace for the world's tourists, lurking beneath the surface is the immutable consciousness that this paradise can be washed away in an instant. But inherent in its residents is a stoic resolve to rebuild and restore at all costs, an attitude that has resulted in the marvel of modern Charleston.

To others she has given of her beauty,
Her gardens, and her dim, old, faded ways,
Her laughter, and her happy, drifting hours,
Glad, spendthrift April, squandering her flowers,
The sharp, still wonder of her Autumn days;
Her chimes that shimmer from St. Michael's steeple
Across the deep maturity of June,
Like sunlight slanting over open water
Under a high, blue, listless afternoon.

Visitor and native can not help but to be astonished at her beauty. This is true not only in the spring, when the bright flood of azaleas cleanse us of lingering winter, but also in November, on gray, wet days when the tiny leaves of the crepe myrtle provide the city's sole fall color. Writers have long remarked on this fact. Fanny Kemble, the English actress, noted in 1838 that "The city is highly picturesque, and although pervaded with an air of decay, it is a genteel infirmity, as might be that of a distressed elderly gentlewoman. It has none of the smug primness of the northern cities but a look of state as of quondam wealth and importance, a little gone down in the world, yet remembering its former dignity."

But when the dusk is deep upon the harbor,
She finds me where her rivers meet and speak,
And while the constellations ride the silence
High overhead, her cheek is on my cheek.

Of all the writers who have turned their pens to Charleston, none more lovingly or accurately captured her than her own son, DuBose Heyward. He was born in the city on August 31, 1885, the year of a cyclone, exactly 365 days prior to the great earthquake. The earthquake of 1886 signaled the nadir of Charleston's fortunes, and she would not recover until after Heyward's death in 1940. It was out of this ruined era that Heyward and numerous others would begin to build an appreciation of the remarkable, poverty-preserved treasure that surrounded them. Many of the initial leaders of the Charleston Renaissance, a literary and artistic movement in the city, were "from away." John Bennett came here from Ohio and mined the region's folk culture. Laura Bragg, from Massachusetts, led The Charleston Museum to a position of independent stature and fostered an awareness of the city's remarkable past. Natives though were unquestionably most adept at capturing the ethereal qualities of the city and the land about it. To this day, no artist has succeeded in more lovingly depicting the city than Alice Smith, who was raised on Church Street. She and her father, D.E.H. Smith, produced a landmark book, *The Dwelling Houses of Charleston*, which was the clarion call for preservation in the city.

Heyward alone gained a national reputation. His poetry, written in the early 1920s, led to a period of prose, with *Porgy* written in 1925. Other novels followed, but the transformation of *Porgy* into play and later to *Porgy and Bess*, capped Heyward's literary career and realized Charleston's re-emergence into the cultural life of the American nation.

I know her in the thrill behind the dark
When sleep brims all her silent thoroughfares.
She is the glamor in the quiet park
That kindles simple things like grass and trees.
Wistful and wanton as her sea-born airs,
Bringer of dim, rich, age-old memories.

Heyward wrote "Dusk," the poem that forms the framework of this introduction, for *Carolina Chansons—Legends of the Lowcountry*, a book of poems that he and Hervey Allen published in 1922. In the introduction to the book, he stated his intention when writing about Charleston and the region: "The South, however, has been 'interpreted' so often, either with condescending pity or nauseous sentimentality, that it is the aim of this book to speak simply and carefully amid a babel of unauthentic utterance." "Dusk" concluded the volume of poems. No son ever penned a more loving song.

Out on the gloom-deep water, when the nights
Are choked with fog, and perilous, and blind,
She is the faith that tends the calling lights.
Hers is the stifled voice of harbor bells
Muffled and broken by the mist and wind.
Hers are the eyes through which I look on life
And find it brave and splendid. And the stir
Of hidden music shaping all my songs,
And these my songs, my all belong to her.

—C. Patton Hash
May 2000

COAST GUARD VESSEL. This ship was used during World War II in Charleston's harbor. The Fort Sumter Hotel is visible in the background.

106 TRADD STREET. This dwelling, seen in its more mature and quiet middle age, shows no sign of a raucous youth. Colonel John Stuart built it between 1767 and 1772. This home would have been the center of a great deal of interesting activity, since the owner was King George III's superintendent of Indian affairs for the Southern colonies. It is likely that the colonel received delegations of American Indians from all over the Southeast—Cherokee, Creek, Choctaw, and others. Stuart remained loyal to the Crown, and this home was the site of much plotting against the rebels. Patriots forced the owner to leave town precipitously in 1775, not long after the house was finished.

A well-established and oft-repeated legend places this home as the one from which Francis Marion jumped to escape his liquor-imbibing comrades. Legend has it that Marion's colleagues locked him in a room on the house's upper floor with the intention of making him join in their revelry. Instead, Marion, a teetotaler, jumped out of the window, injured his leg, and was carried to his plantation in upper Berkeley County. There he was able to avoid British capture after the fall of Charles Town and thus became the famed partisan leader.

SOUTH OF BROAD

No section of Charleston is more mystically regarded than the tree-shaded tip of the peninsula that lies "south of Broad Street." Broad is essentially the social dividing line. To live below it is to have; to live above it is to remain somehow unfulfilled. One may have a gracious home, in a lovely "suburb" of the city, yet feel a deep and secret envy for the resident of the most narrow dwelling a stone's throw from the Battery. Visitors are rarely in Charleston for more than a few moments before the term, or more likely the shorthand "S.O.B.," is used in some manner or another,

often complimentary, sometimes not. Frequently used phrases often evolve from witticism to cliche, only a few pass into perpetual truth. So it is with the lasting reputation of this neighborhood.

It is a well-earned regard. The area consists of the largest portion of the original land division made in the city. Half of the ancient walled city lies below Broad Street. Many of the city's oldest residences are found here, particularly in the first two blocks of Tradd Street and several of the central blocks of Church Street. Most importantly, the Battery is here, long the choice

social gathering place of Charlestonians. Running along the eastern portion of the peninsula's tip is the "High Battery," an extraordinary row of palatial townhouses that look out over the sea wall, across the harbor, and to the Atlantic beyond, a sight unlike any other in the country. At one time significant portions of the area had commercial uses, as these photographs show, though retail trade is now found in other parts of the city and the ships that used the old docks are now berthed elsewhere.

THE BATTERY. Local photographers Osborn and Durbec took this photograph in the summer of 1860.

EAST AND SOUTH BATTERY. In the foreground of this photograph are the remains of one of the 12.75-inch rifled guns that George Alfred Trenholm gave to the Confederate cause in 1863. Confederates mounted one at the foot of Cumberland Street, and the other in this battery at the corner of East and South Battery. Known as Blakely rifles, they could fire shells weighing between 470 and 650 pounds. They had a range of 6,600 feet when firing a 470-pound shell. Yet they served very little military purpose, as Union forces remained out of their range. When the Confederates evacuated the city, they resolved to leave no war materiel, and retreating forces blew up the guns. The explosion blew huge fragments into the air, with one landing on the roof of the Roper House three doors away. The massive gun carriage for this "monster gun" is seen in the middle of the street.

4 SOUTH BATTERY. Many formidable women have made their mark on the history of Charleston, helping to shape the city's unique character. Few were as colorful as Margaret Rose Anthony Julia Josephine Catherine Cornelia Donovan O'Donovan Breaux Simonds Gummeré Calhoun, better known as Daisy Breaux. A native of New Orleans, she, it would not be unfair to say, imbibed some of that city's Gallic theatrical nature before marrying Andrew Simonds of Charleston. *The Autobiography of a Chameleon*, a splendid first-person account of her life, details her many adventures, from birth to "sub-deb"-hood through three marriages. Mrs. Simonds Gummeré Calhoun entertained many notables there during her tenure, including Confederate generals, Navy admirals, Spanish–American war heroes, and President Theodore Roosevelt. In 1905, the house was sold and later converted to an inn known as Villa Margherita.

13

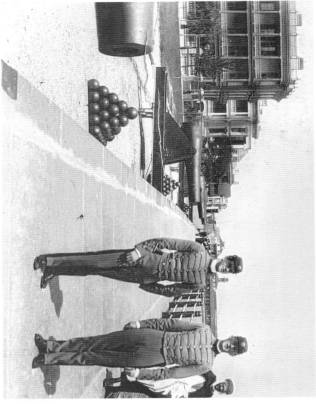

FORT SUMTER HOTEL. The influx of tourists in the 1920s necessitated the construction of modern facilities for their lodging. Completed in 1923, the Fort Sumter Hotel boasted that it was Charleston's "only waterfront hotel" with "spacious lobbies, sun parlors and terraces" and rooms that were "comfortably and luxuriously furnished." A signpost with distances to various far off cities in front of the hotel was a favorite location for photo-takers. George Gershwin stayed here during a portion of his visit to the city while writing *Porgy and Bess*. The hotel was converted into condominiums in 1974.

THE BATTERY. This photograph shows two proud Citadel cadets at the Battery. It appears to have been taken sometime after the federal government loaned the Confederate cannon, seen in the background, to the city in 1900.

THE BATTERY AND WHITE POINT GARDENS. Snow is an infrequent guest in Charleston. These photographs were taken after the snow of February 1899, which blanketed the entire state. Snowfall amounts ranged from 2 inches in Charleston to 18 inches farther inland.

BATTERY ROW. "On certain days he would turn to the south when he left the court, and soon would emerge into a land of such beauty that he never lost the illusion that it was unreal. No one seemed to work in that country, except the happy, well-clothed negroes who frequently came to back gates when he passed, and gave him tender morsels from the white folk's kitchens. The great gleaming houses looked out at him with kindly eyes that peered between solid walls of climbing roses. Ladies on the deep piazzas would frequently send a servant running out to give him a coin and speed him on his way."
(DuBose Heyward, *Porgy*, 1925.)

BATTERY ROW, C. 1865. This splendid row of homes on the Battery is shown at the conclusion of the Civil War. The Union bombardment of the city scarred each of these houses. The Daniel Heyward house in the right foreground was one of the permanent casualties. The former Drayton residence now stands on the site, at the corner of Atlantic and East Battery Streets.

HIGH BATTERY. The High Battery is shown here, absorbing the 13-foot waves and 106-mile-per-hour winds of the 1911 storm. The Missroon House and buildings along Southern Wharf are seen through the spray of the waves.

A PORTION OF THE FORTIFICATION. Charleston defense armament at White Point Gardens is shown here after the close of the Civil War. Although no longer standing today, the tall light post, visible in the background in the center of White Point Gardens, survived the war.

8 SOUTH BATTERY. Built around 1768, this elegant frame dwelling was the southernmost residence in the city by the time of the Revolution. The home passed into the hands of Revolutionary patriot and presidential cousin William Washington in 1782. He and his family owned the home for almost 50 years, before Henry Gourdin purchased it.

The original entrance to the house was found not on the South Battery facade, seen in this image, but facing Church Street. Later landfill projects enabled expansion of the lot and reorientation of the house as shown here.

56 SOUTH BATTERY. A large, Romantic-era balcony covers this early-nineteenth-century dwelling at 56 South Battery, giving it a Creole-like appearance. The large palm tree shown in this picture, now sadly gone, added to its tropical appearance. The house was built around 1800, and the same family has owned it since 1887.

64 South Battery. When William Gibbes constructed 64 South Battery about 1772, this home had the benefit of a wonderful view of the Ashley River. A large wharf nearly 300 feet in length, one of the most modern of colonial Charles Town, warehouses, and other buildings combined to make a very impressive site on the southern tip of the city's peninsula. The Roebling family of Brooklyn Bridge fame purchased the house in 1928. Significant restoration of the dwelling and redesign of the garden ensued.

68 SOUTH BATTERY. John Harth, a planter with interest in rice mills, built this home around 1800. A later owner, Thomas Legare, covered the frame house in stucco. After his death, it was sold to Henry Augustus Middleton, a rice planter with extensive holdings north of the city in Georgetown District and south along the Combahee River in Beaufort District. Prior to the Civil War, Middleton and his family spent their summers in Newport, Rhode Island, a practice common among wealthy planter families in the South. The Middleton family sold the house in the 1920s to the Pettus family from Maryland. The Pettuses completed an extensive renovation of both the residence and the garden (seen here), shortly after their purchase.

21 EAST BATTERY. Charles Edmondston built this house about 1820, soon after the completion of the seawall on East Battery. A severe economic depression in 1837 ruined Edmondston, forcing him to sell it to William Alston of the Miles Brewton House on King Street. Alston then gave the dwelling to his son Charles, who refashioned the home in the Greek Revival style. Note the elaborate panel on the house's parapet displaying the Alston family arms.

From this vantage point General Beauregard watched a portion of the bombardment of Fort Sumter. Later in 1861 Robert E. Lee moved here on the evening of the Great Fire, when the blaze threatened the Mills House.

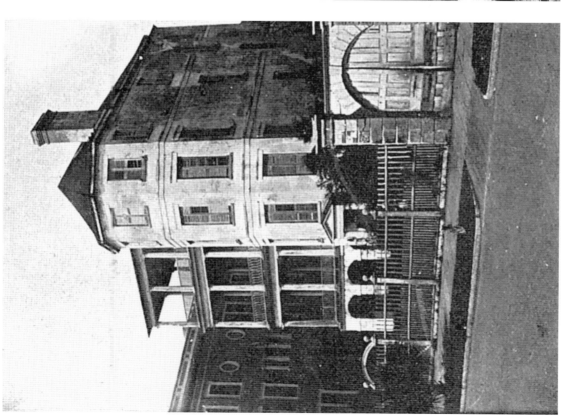

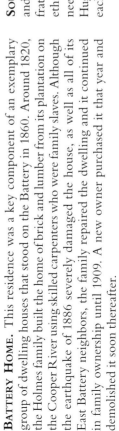

SOUTH CAROLINA SOCIETY HALL. The hall, located at 72 Meeting Street and designed by Gabriel Manigault, serves as home to the city's third oldest fraternal organization. The South Carolina Society dates from an era when ethnic groups organized themselves to care for their fellow-countrymen's needs and enjoy the pleasure of social intercourse. In this case, French Huguenots, Protestants forced to flee Roman Catholic France, paid a small due each time they met, earning it the original name of the "Two Bit Club."

BATTERY HOME. This residence was a key component of an exemplary group of dwelling houses that stood on the Battery in 1860. Around 1820, the Holmes family built the home of brick and lumber from its plantation on the Cooper River using skilled carpenters who were family slaves. Although the earthquake of 1886 severely damaged the house, as well as all of its East Battery neighbors, the family repaired the dwelling and it continued in family ownership until 1909. A new owner purchased it that year and demolished it soon thereafter.

23

7 MEETING STREET. Merchant Josiah Smith built this home immediately after the American Revolution. Smith was involved in the slave trade in the colonial era, and records show that he received 11 cargoes of slaves in South Carolina. Because he was an ardent Continental patriot, the British exiled Smith to St. Augustine. His diary of the experience provides a valuable record of the sacrifices of almost 30 American leaders exiled there after the fall of Charles Town in 1780. Smith lived to the age of 95, passing away in February 1826, almost 50 years after the signing of the Declaration of Independence.

35 MEETING STREET. The colony's first royal lieutenant governor, William Bull, built this residence. He served the colony and Crown in a number of offices during his public career, including lieutenant governor and acting governor. His son, William Bull Jr., was the first native South Carolinian to hold a medical degree, but like his father, he held many public offices, including that of lieutenant governor. William Bull served as acting governor five times. When the rebels took over the government, Bull retired to his estate outside of Charles Town, where he remained until banished in 1777. Bull returned during the British occupation of the city, but left with the King's departing troops, never to return.

18 MEETING STREET. Of all of the city's architectural styles, none was more suited to the Charleston single house than the Adamesque style. The style is derived from two Scottish brothers, Robert and James Adam, who used classical precedents found in Roman domestic architecture, particularly in the excavated ruins of Pompeii at the foot of Mount Vesuvius. It marked a distinct change in eighteenth-century architectural fashion, which previously had been based on the architecture of Roman temples. The Adam brothers used the interplay of diverse geometric shapes for the design of rooms, and airy plaster and paint decoration to distinguish their work from the popular Palladian style.

This new fashion reached Charleston just after the Revolution and local builders reinterpreted it to fit the city's needs. These dwelling houses with exteriors of simple dignity, a delicately classic piazza screen, and the gentle sway of the piazzas' elliptical arches created a house type that is still unsurpassed in the city. The home of Thomas Heyward Jr. at 18 Meeting Street, built around 1803, is a superlative example of this brilliant era.

16 MEETING STREET. With 24,000 square feet, the residence that George Walton Williams built at 16 Meeting Street in 1876 was the largest home to be constructed in the city after the Civil War. Williams made a fortune in a number of different business, including importing, banking, and even blockade running. A daughter who inherited the house married Patrick Calhoun, grandson of John C. Calhoun. Later owners converted the house into an inn named the Calhoun Mansion.

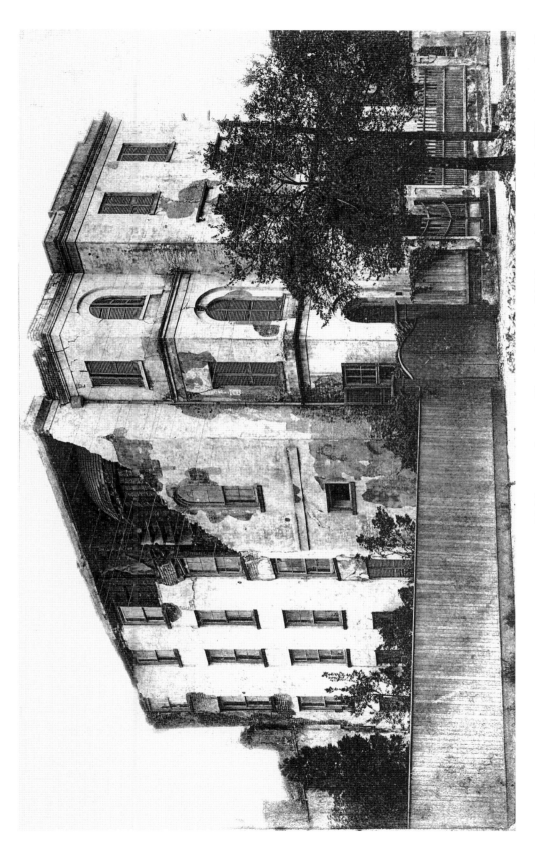

26 MEETING STREET. The earthquake of 1886 severely damaged the William Mason Smith House. All four walls of the house needed extensive repairs, the total damage estimate coming to about $8,500. On the official report that listed each building, in the category entitled "What should be done to make it safe," the engineer reported "By rebuilding it."

59 MEETING STREET. Merchant Benjamin Savage built this home between 1747 and 1750, though residents and members have known it for years as the Branford-Horry House. Savage's niece, Elizabeth Savage, who later married William Branford, inherited the house. Elias Horry, a grandson, forms the other half of the house's name. Horry was the president of the South Carolina Canal and Railroad Company, which operated the longest railroad in the world in the 1830s, from Charleston to Hamburg, South Carolina, 131 miles in distance. He is credited with adding the home's piazzas over Meeting Street, which have sheltered a bus stop for generations, perhaps the most elegant in the nation.

Immediately to the right of this home is the property's old stable. It was adapted into a residence in the early twentieth century and was the home of federal judge Waites Waring. Judge Waring wrote many important judicial opinions in the civil rights movement's early days, most significantly a dissent that formed the basis of the Supreme Court's later ruling on *Brown v. Board of Education.*

FIRST SCOTS PRESBYTERIAN CHURCH. Built around 1814, First Scots Presbyterian Church, at the corner of Meeting and Tradd Streets, is the fifth oldest church structure in the city. Unique in Charleston with its two towers, First Scots is variously described as being inspired by Benjamin Latrobe's Roman Catholic Cathedral in Baltimore or by the work of Robert and James Adam in England. Scottish members of the older Independent or Congregational Church, now known as the Circular Congregational Church, founded First Scots.

Note in the foreground the streetlight suspended over Meeting Street, a frequently targeted object of a "genteel" group of young men that once frequented Pete's Grocery, which was immediately across the street from the church. The boys would also use lard from a barrel in the store to grease the streetcar tracks. Upon reaching this point on the route, the streetcar would lose traction and become the target of a barrage of fireworks shot from the front windows of Pete's.

FIRST BAPTIST CHURCH. Regarded as the "Mother Church" of the Southern Baptist denomination, Charleston's First Baptist Church at number 61 Church Street has its roots with a congregation organized in Kittery, Maine, in 1682. Persecution by Puritans in New England forced them to immigrate to Carolina, where they established themselves as one of the five earliest congregations in the colony.

Robert Mills designed this church in 1822 in a bold form of the Greek Revival style. He described it in a later book as "the best specimen of correct taste in architecture of the modern buildings of this city."

To the north stands 69 Church, known as the Capers-Motte House, built around 1750. The Smith family lived here at the time the picture was taken in 1927. The most famous member of that talented clan was the artist Alice Ravenel Huger Smith, whose watercolors are considered to be a high point of the Charleston Renaissance. A subsequent owner removed the piazzas seen on the dwelling.

27 KING STREET. This house is perhaps Charleston's most splendidly preserved private residence, with a chain of ownership that reaches within several related families to the builder in 1769. Miles Brewton, a merchant and slave trader, constructed this home that represents the height of Georgian architectural styling, not only in Charles Town, but throughout Great Britain and her empire. Josiah Quincy of Boston wrote in 1773, "Dined with considerable company at Miles Brewton, Esqr's, a gentleman of very large fortune: a most superb house said to have cost him 8,000 of sterling. The grandest hall I ever beheld, azure blue satin window curtains, rich blue paper with gilt, mashee borders, most elegant pictures, excessive grand and costly looking glasses, etc."

In 1775 Brewton and his entire family were lost at sea while on a voyage to Philadelphia. The home passed to Brewton's sister, Rebecca Motte, during whose ownership the British used it as their headquarters while occupying Charles Town. Later, at the end of the Civil War, the Union army used the residence for the same purpose.

CHURCH STREET. Few homes in the city come near the beauty of this extraordinary grouping of three single houses on Church Street. Number 90, nearest in the foreground, was constructed about 1760. Its neighbor to the north, now the rectory of St. Philip's Church, was built in the first decade of the nineteenth century, while the third home, number 94, is the earliest of the three, dating to 1755. Together they show the variety and versatility of the traditional house plan popular in the city for almost 200 years.

COATES ROW. These four picturesque buildings are known as Coates Row, named for a sea captain who owned the range by 1806. Captain Coates's wife operated a popular coffee shop on Tradd Street. In the 1790s the French Jacobin Club of Charleston held its meetings in the row. For much of the life of Coates Row, which is just south of the Old Exchange Building, there has been a purveyor of spirits, sometimes legal, sometimes not, on the premises. Extensive wine cellars are located beneath the buildings. It is a cherished Charleston business tradition that survives to this day.

33

8 ST. MICHAEL'S ALLEY. Charleston's smallest buildings are often its most lovely ones. This is certainly true of the former law office of James Louis Petigru at 8 St. Michael's Alley, shown in the center of the photograph. It is not an ordinary attorney who has the city's premier architect design his office, but of course, Petigru was anything but ordinary.

Petigru was born in the same town as John C. Calhoun—Abbeville, South Carolina—though they were political and philosophical opponents until Calhoun's death in 1851. Elected state attorney general in 1822, Petigru held only one other elected office (state representative) and one appointed office (federal attorney for South Carolina) for the remainder of his life. Yet, friends and opponents alike regarded him as the state's premier private citizen, a stalwart voice of moderation and Unionism. Because of this esteem, Petigru could speak without fear on issues considered too volatile by others.

CABBAGE ROW. Known to early-twentieth-century Charlestonians as "Cabbage Row," 89 Church Street, built about 1783, was a "negro tenement" at the time this photograph was taken. Residents sold vegetables and other commodities from the windows. The quality of the tenants apparently attracted attention from the police; law enforcement called there frequently. Novelist Dubose Heyward, who lived at 76 Church Street, was also attracted to the activities of his neighbors. Cabbage Row, with some literary changes, provided the backdrop of the most famous American opera of all time. These photographs were taken just after Heyward's novel was published and just before the building's restoration.

36

RAINBOW ROW. Looking south along East Bay Street is Rainbow Row in its infancy. This photograph was taken by architect Albert Simons, who was responsible for much of the restoration that would take place along this famed row of homes. The word "infancy" is used because the name "Rainbow Row" and its current appearance dates only to the 1930s, when early preservationists took an interest in its future. The first couple to restore a home, Judge and Mrs. Lionel Legge, painted their home a brilliant pink, a custom that subsequent restorers followed when decking their residences in other pastel colors.

RAINBOW ROW. A portion of Rainbow Row on East Bay is shown here just before it gained its famous colors and name. These homes represent the typical eighteenth- and early nineteenth-century combination of commercial and residential functions, a practice from which developed the renowned single house. Merchants maintained stores on the street level of their homes and their domestic quarters on the upper floors. Many of the owners of these structures were Scottish merchants, including the Gordon, Deas, Dulles, and Tunno families.

ADGER'S WHARVES. Like much of the rest of the city, by the beginning of the twentieth century Charleston's port facilities were dilapidated at best. The deterioration began before the Civil War as the city's residents turned their focus inward and New York assumed the role of the central port for Atlantic shipping.

There were some efforts on the part of the maritime industry to reassert Charleston's place in the world market. Irish-born James Adger bought several of the older wharves in the early 1840s, modernized them, and established a shipping line that competed with Northern rivals. He constructed a series of buildings to serve as warehouses and offices and paved the wharf with cobblestones.

In the early 1920s the state established a ports commission to place the wharf facilities under central control and re-establish Charleston as the preeminent port on the lower Atlantic Seaboard, particularly for shipping from Panama. These photographs of Adger's Wharves were taken after the commission assumed control of the historic property.

T W O

DOWNTOWN

To describe the vast commercial heart of Charleston, we have carved out a large district. Shaped like a fishhook, it begins at the intersection of King and Calhoun, runs along King to Broad, and then east on Broad until it reaches East Bay. There it turns north and ends at the Customs House. For the sake of convenience, Meeting Street, above Broad and below Calhoun, is included in this zone.

While there is no historic precedent for such an arrangement, this area encompasses the retail, wholesale, and professional center of the city.

Here are most of the shops, stores, warehouses, printers, hotels, and public buildings. Several churches and buildings with social purposes are also included.

BROAD STREET. A more vibrant block of Broad is shown here than the one below, looking toward St. Michael's Church. To the left are the offices of the Equitable Insurance Company, next to the law offices of Mayor Thomas P. Stoney, at 51 Broad Street. The large sign for Becker's Drugstore can be seen farther down the street. Both photos were taken by the same individual at the same time.

40

RUTLEDGE HOUSE. John Rutledge, South Carolina's indispensable patriot, built this home about 1765, creating a handsome companion to its neighbor at 114 Broad. Rutledge served the state as its first chief executive and then after an intervening term, he held the position again, this time with almost dictatorial powers due to the British occupation of Charles Town. For this he gained the nickname "Dictator John." One of the signatories to the Constitution, Rutledge served the new republic as Supreme Court senior associate justice and subsequently as chief justice.

Another owner, Robert Goodwyn Rhett, a mayor of Charleston, entertained many notables in the house, including President William Howard Taft. Rhett's butler, William Deas, invented a special dish, She-crab soup, to commemorate the presidential visit.

PEOPLE'S BUILDING. While much of the "modern" era bypassed Charleston, here and there certain "intrusions" occurred. The builders at 18 Broad Street constructed what they touted as "the only strictly modern office building in the city," in the most current architectural style. When completed in 1911 the People's Building cost a total of $300,000 and towered over much of the city; its only rivals in stature were nearby St. Michael's and St. Philip's and the uptown steeple of St. Matthew's Lutheran Church.

President William Howard Taft visited the city to help inaugurate the building. Apparently aware of a local debate on the appropriateness of the structure and its scale, Taft was heard to comment, "I don't believe that it ruined the skyline, but if it did the view from up here makes it worth it."

180 BROAD STREET. The rules of war changed dramatically from the outbreak of the Civil War in Charleston harbor in 1861 until Sherman's march through South Carolina in early 1865. In 1863 Union forces on Morris Island constructed a battery that began firing into the city in August, initiating a bombardment that continued for the remainder of the war. Much of the old city below Calhoun Street was in range of the guns, and few buildings escaped without some damage. Horrified that civilians were under military fire, Confederates scrambled to find some way to stop the shelling. At one point five Union generals were quartered in this house at 180 Broad Street, well within the bombed district. This move caused Union forces to retaliate, quartering 600 Confederate officers on Morris Island in range of Confederate artillery. The shelling continued by both sides until the city fell in February 1865.

SHEPHEARD'S TAVERN. For more than 200 years this was "The Corner," a political and social gathering place of immense significance to the city. Shepheard's Tavern, located at the corner of Church and Broad Streets, was believed to be the second tavern building that stood at the location. Social clubs, fraternal organizations, and political gatherings were held at Shepheard's, including many of the meetings connected with the Stamp Act protest and later the Revolution. Anti-Stamp Act partisans built a gallows at the intersection of Church and Broad with the words "Liberty and No Stamp Act" inscribed on it. An effigy of the tax collector swung below.

Most importantly, this building was the meeting place for the inaugural meeting of the first masonic lodge in the American colonies in 1736. The Scottish Rite of Freemasons regard the building as their birthplace, where their organization met for the first time on May 31, 1801.

41

42

CHARLESTON: ALONE AMONG THE CITIES

BROAD STREET. This 1927 view shows most of the southern side of the block between East Bay and Church Streets. The street, despite its reputation as "the Wall Street of the South," looks strangely deserted. In the center of the photograph is 19 Broad, home of the *News & Courier* for 55 years. Known famously around the city and state as the "Old Lady of Broad Street," the newspaper staunchly defended the values of the old city against the rising tide of Upcountry power. The newspaper garnered its only Pulitzer Prize, for the editorial writing of Robert Lathan, the year this photograph was taken. The following year the paper moved to a new building located on the site of South Carolina Institute Hall at 134 Meeting Street.

OLD EXCHANGE BUILDING. This is a view of the Old Exchange Building at the foot of Broad Street, as it appeared immediately after the Civil War. Note the palmetto in the right foreground. Charleston had few palmettos along public streets in that era. Residents planted several at the time of the Secession Crisis, but Northern photographers combing the city for views after the war ended often pictured this tree with the caption "The only palmetto tree in Charleston."

114 BROAD STREET. Not only is this home a neoclassical jewel, but in terms of dimensions, it is one of Charleston's most palatial residences. Colonel Thomas Pinckney Jr. completed the house soon after construction commenced in 1829. The lofty ceilings (18 feet) of the first floor afforded occupants a substantial amount of ventilation, while a unique T-shaped floor plan allowed for ease in entertaining. Rosetta Ella Pinckney sold the house to the Roman Catholic Diocese of Charleston in 1866, and the Catholic church has used it since that time as the bishop's residence.

43

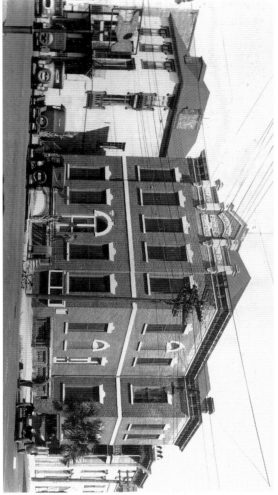

JAMES LOUIS PETIGRU HOME. The damage to the city resulting from the fire of 1861 is apparent in this view of Broad Street looking east. In the foreground to the left is the ruin of James Louis Petigru's home. Just past it is the tower of St. John and St. Finbar, the magnificent Roman Catholic cathedral destroyed in the disaster.

50 BROAD STREET. Originally built as the office of the Bank of South Carolina, this structure housed the Charleston Library Society from 1836 until 1914. The Library Society sold it to the Charleston Chamber of Commerce, which had its offices here when the photograph was taken.

DuBose Heyward's inspiration for his protagonist "Porgy," Sammy Smalls, used to loiter with his cart on the Church Street sidewalk alongside the building.

CITY HALL. The second oldest city hall in use in the United States, after that of New York City, Charleston's municipal center is yet another building that her famous amateur architect, Gabriel Manigault, designed. Originally built as the office of the first Bank of the United States in 1800, it became City Hall in 1818.

INTERIOR OF CITY HALL. The appearance of the council chambers is virtually unchanged from soon after the earthquake. Shown here is a magnificent collection of portraits, including the impressive portrait of Washington (at right) that Jonathan Trumbull painted to commemorate the first president's visit in 1791. The large portrait to the left of Washington's is of James Monroe, who came to Charleston in part to participate in the dedication of the new City Hall. Samuel F.B. Morse, famed inventor of the telegraph, painted the portrait.

CHARLESTON COUNTY COURTHOUSE. One of the most significant buildings in the United States, the Charleston County Courthouse, at Meeting and Broad Streets, is shown here in the midst of a long period of neglect. The building incorporates the walls of South Carolina's colonial statehouse, which burned in 1788. It was here that the first reading of the Declaration of Independence in the state took place.

After the fire, architect James Hoban was involved in the effort to rebuild and enlarge the structure as a county courthouse. The State also hired Hoban, a native of Dublin, to build the new statehouse in Columbia. It is generally believed that he met George Washington while the president toured the Southern states, perhaps explaining why Hoban designed the White House in the District of Columbia. Architectural historians since have noted the similarity between the two buildings' style and design.

An extensive renovation in 1883 significantly altered the building. Later additions, made about the time this photo was taken and in 1941, made the building awkward to use and lessened interest in its preservation. By the time of Hurricane Hugo in 1989, the County had to undertake a complete restoration of the building.

159 MEETING STREET. Founded in 1860 with $500 in capital, C.D. Franke and Company grew into one of Victorian Charleston's most extensive businesses. This shows the Franke establishment when it was located at 159 Meeting Street. Originally serving as a coach and wagon maker, the company, as evidenced by its delivery truck in the left foreground of the photo, served the automotive needs of Charlestonians as that age dawned. Franke was a native of Kurnik, Prussia, and came to the city about 1853. By 1884 his company was making $60,000 a year in sales. Franke's motto was "uebung macht den meister," or "Practice makes the master."

FOUR CORNERS OF LAW. Shown here are two of the four corners (with a sliver of the third) of the intersection of Meeting and Broad Streets, Charleston's most important crossroads. The steeple of St. Michael's Episcopal Church, the city's oldest religious building, completed in 1761, towers over the scene. During the Civil War the steeple served as Augustine Smythe's "lofty perch," from which he monitored Union movements on the islands.

The row of quoins and the corner of the building to the left is the Charleston County Courthouse.

POST-WAR MEETING STREET. War's ruin is nowhere more apparent than here on Meeting Street immediately after the Civil War. Though the fire of 1861, which was not war related, caused the damage seen in this image, the inability to rebuild after the catastrophe is directly attributable to the conflict. In the foreground are the steps to the Charleston Theatre, which hosted many happy events in its 20-some years of existence. Scaffolding encases the steeple and ruins of Circular Church, which would be rebuilt in more modest form 30 years later.

GUARD HOUSE. Seen here after the earthquake of 1886, the Guard House, designed by Charles Reichardt (the architect of the Charleston Hotel), proved to be one of the city's permanent losses to the disaster. The Guard House served as the city's police station and the location of the mayor's court.

150 MEETING STREET. Circular Church was nearing completion of its third building when this photograph was taken around 1893. Architects loosely based the church's design on an eleventh-century church in Cologne, Germany, which is also three sided.

To the left of the church is the site of South Carolina Institute Hall, which burned in the 1861 fire. Across the street, the three-arched structure forms the entrance to O'Neill's Opera House; the theatre space is the large structure immediately behind.

ST. CHARLES HOTEL. The hotel at the corner of Hasell and Meeting Street went through several name changes in its lifetime, including the Argyle, and later, the St. Charles. In 1899 the hotel reserved its rooms solely for the use of ladies attending the Confederate reunion.

MEETING STREET. Shown in this picture of Meeting Street is the side of the Fireproof Building, the rear of City Hall, St. Michael's Episcopal Church, and on the right side of the street, the Timrod Hotel. Next door to the Timrod, in the brick house, was the Anchor Bar. Located near the city's renowned "Four Corners" of government, the bar served as a vital refreshment center for Charleston's public servants. The Timrod and the Anchor Bar are now sadly gone, replaced with the county office building.

FIREPROOF BUILDING. Architect Robert Mills promoted himself as the first native-born and native-trained architect in the American republic, because his contemporaries were either natives of Europe, were educated there, or had traveled abroad. In 1820 Mills was appointed state architect and began work on a series of buildings, including courthouses and jails throughout the state and a state office building in Charleston. Construction on the building at 100 Meeting Street began in 1822 and was not complete until 1827. It was the first building in the nation to have fireproof rooms to store official records. Most of the materials used in the building were non-flammable, including iron window frames and shutters, stone floors, and a copper roof. Today it houses the South Carolina Historical Society.

WASHINGTON PARK. Located in the center of the historic city, Washington Park is familiar to generations of Charlestonians as "City Hall Park." Named in honor of Washington on the centennial anniversary of the Battle of Yorktown, the park is filled with monuments and tablets to war heroes, a poet, a president's mother, and a Freemason, among others. Shown here is the monument to General Beauregard, who so gallantly and cleverly defended the city from Union troops during the Civil War. Beauregard, whose Creole nature blended well with Charleston's sensibilities, was rarely without an ingenious plan to thwart the enemy. Arthur Fremantle, a British army observer, noted that the Louisianian planned to cover Fort Sumter in Spanish moss to cushion the blows of the attacking Union ironclads. No evidence shows that he actually carried out his plan.

A tablet commemorating Francis Salvador, the first Jew to hold public office in the United States and the first to die for the American nation during the Revolution, is on the wall behind the young ladies sitting on the bench. The home of Daniel Ravenel is in the background. Since its construction around 1800, nearly all of the owners have been named Daniel Ravenel; the land on which the home stands has been in the family since the mid-eighteenth century.

SOUTH CAROLINA INSTITUTE HALL. This photograph was taken on May 10, 1860, from the roof of the Mills House looking down at Meeting Street. The large building, South Carolina Institute Hall, in the center, appears quiet. Yet only a few days previous, it had been the site of one of the most tumultuous meetings in American history. A group of pro-secessionist South Carolina politicians called "fire-eaters," working with delegates from Alabama, forced a platform fight over probable-nominee Stephen Douglas's stand on free-soil sovereignty at the Democratic convention. When defeated, Southern delegates walked out of the convention on April 30. Two separate meetings, one of mostly Northern delegates, the other of Southern, resulted in two nominees for the Democratic party. This split ensured the election of Republican candidate Abraham Lincoln.

Institute Hall continued as a witness to the great tragedy when it played a central role in the final momentous act of 1860. After Lincoln's election, South Carolina elected a convention to consider secession from the Union. Originally it met in Columbia, but delegates removed to Charleston because of a small pox outbreak in the capital. The convention passed the Ordinance of Secession unanimously on December 20, 1860, in a closed-door session at St. Andrew's Hall on Broad Street. Later that evening the convention reassembled in Institute Hall for a public signing ceremony. As their names were called, each delegate came forward to sign the document in front of thousands of their fellow citizens.

Almost a year later on the evening of December 11, 1861, a fire destroyed Institute Hall, Circular Church next door, and much of central Charleston.

53

DEUTSCHE FREUNDSCHAFTS BUND HALL. Located at the corner of Meeting and George Streets, this structure serves as a reminder of the powerful influence of Charleston's German community. From the 1730s onward, significant numbers of Germans lived in the city, and their involvement in civic activities was manifested in their founding of a number of organizations including the German Friendly Society, the Arion Society, the German Artillery (among other military units), and four Lutheran churches on the peninsula. A German-language newspaper was in print from 1853 until 1917, and at least one Lutheran church continued to worship in German until 1924. The Deutsche Freundschafts Bund was a literary and social fellowship society of German immigrants in the nineteenth century. This building later housed other German societies, and during World War II, the U.S.O. It is now the home of the Washington Light Infantry.

WILLIAM BURROWS HOUSE. Burrows was a native of England who prospered immensely in Carolina. Active in the social affairs of the colony, he was president of the St. George Society, steward of the South Carolina Society, and one of the founders of the Library Society. At his death, he owned more than 10,000 acres of land and this splendid home at 71 Broad Street, which he had built between 1772 and 1774.

William Ward Burrows, son of the owner, served gallantly in the Revolution. After the conflict, he was appointed the first commandant of the Marine Corps in 1798. He sold the home to Jehu Jones, who converted the home and the outbuildings into a hotel, regarded as the finest establishment of its type in Charleston in the early nineteenth century. Jones was a free person of color, a status of a precarious nature in the city. Though these individuals were technically free, they were protected by the barest of civil rights and governed by an entirely separate set of laws. Despite this, he attained a position of great esteem in the city and hosted many notable lodgers, including Samuel B. Morse.

The house continued in its adopted role as a hotel until the time of the Civil War. After the war it degenerated into a rooming house. In the 1920s a buyer purchased the home with the intention of dismantling it and then reconstructing the house outside of Charleston. While it was taken down, the economic crash of 1929 prevented rebuilding. The dismantled parts of the house were in storage for many years before the drawing room and dining room were reconstructed at Winterthur in Delaware.

56

200 MEETING STREET. Seen in this never-before-published 1860 photograph, the Charleston Hotel was the city's premier hostelry for nearly 100 years. Prussian architect Charles Reichardt designed the hotel, which hosted many notable guests, including Daniel Webster, Jenny Lind, and Princess Louise, a daughter of Queen Victoria. In 1850 the first Christmas tree was erected in honor of hotel guest Jenny Lind.

The hotel was erected as part of an effort to recover from the debilitating recessions of the 1820s and the loss of western cotton markets to Savannah and New Orleans. Construction began in 1838; state funds helped to finance construction, while the City made improvements to Hayne Street, which ran alongside the hotel.

Seen farther down Meeting Street are the steeples of the Circular Church and St. Michael's.

MILLS HOUSE. Another premier antebellum hostelry in Charleston was the establishment of Otis Mills on Meeting Street. Built about 12 years after the construction of the Charleston Hotel, the Mills House represented changing styles in the 1850s. Five stories tall, it had 125 rooms and cost $200,000 to build.

Robert E. Lee maintained his headquarters here while assigned to Charleston. He watched the Great Fire of 1861 from a balcony until the flames came too close and forced him to abandon the hotel. Employees saved the building from destruction by hanging wet blankets out of the windows; the fire, burning just across the street, caused little damage to it.

The hotel saw a long decline after the war's end. In the early twentieth century, owners changed the name to the St. John's Hotel. Records of the vice commission indicate that hotel bellboys and desk clerks conducted a healthy business of another nature while on duty at the hotel. The building was in such disrepair by the late 1960s that owners deemed it necessary to take it down, and rebuild another, taller structure on the site. The new hotel continues under the name of the famous old establishment and with the same iron balcony and general appearance.

CONVENT OF OUR LADY OF MERCY. This convent that stood behind the Cathedral of St. John the Baptist had its origins in the day of John England, South Carolina's first Roman Catholic bishop. In his first years here, Bishop England sought to aid the victims of yellow fever. The first nuns arrived here in 1829, and a year later they opened a school named the Academy of Our Lady of Mercy. The order was involved in hospital work (St. Francis Xavier) and orphanages, one in Charleston and St. Joseph's in Sumter. One of their school buildings was the house at 51 Meeting, which Nathaniel Russell built. That school served as the real-life basis of the fictional convent that Careen O'Hara, the sister of Scarlett, joined in *Gone with the Wind*. This structure, built in 1909 and later torn down in 1972 for townhouses, was used as a school and a convent-college.

HIBERNIAN HALL. Located at 105 Meeting Street and built between 1839 and 1841 at the cost of $40,000, Hibernian Hall is the home of another of Charleston's venerable ethnic societies, the Irish. Thomas U. Walter, who later gained fame for his dome on the Capitol Building in Washington, designed the structure.

In early 1861 the legislature temporarily moved the seat of government to Charleston and met in Hibernian Hall. While the legislature was meeting here, they adopted as the state flag the design that has since been used by South Carolina.

CONNELLEY'S FUNERAL HOME. Shown here are two photographs related to Connelley's Funeral Home, located at 309 Meeting Street. The owner, Jesse M. Connelley, South Carolina's first licensed mortician, established himself as the city's finest provider of funeral services. His business included greenhouses, stables (seen left), the funeral home, a coffin storage facility, and even a tropical fish business. The Horlbeck family built an appropriately somber vine-covered house in 1796; it was converted from mortuary to residential use in 1984.

The photograph above was made to advertise Connelley's automobile services in the era after World War II. It ran frequently in the *News & Courier* during that time.

RADCLIFFE-KING HOUSE. Thomas Radcliffe built this house about 1800 at the corner of Meeting and George Streets, and it was the site of many famous balls while owned by both the builders' family and later by Judge Mitchell King. In 1880 the City purchased the home and converted it into the High School of Charleston. In 1938, after the City moved the school to new quarters on Rutledge Avenue, the house was demolished to build a gymnasium for the College of Charleston.

DANIEL BLAKE'S TENEMENTS. Built before 1772 on a street known as Court House Square, the tenements served as rental property for the wealthy Blake. The corner of the County Court House, on the right side of the picture, housed the office of Sheriff Poulnot in 1927. Across the street on the first floor of the old Hebrew Orphanage was the Rathskeller, another local watering hole. Local politician J.C. Long had his office above that establishment on the second floor.

St. John's Lutheran Church. Located on Archdale Street, St. John's Lutheran Church punctuates this view looking east on Magazine Street. The name of the street is derived from a gunpowder-storage facility that was located nearby at the time of the Revolution.

Unitarian Church. Note the earthquake damage to the spire of the Unitarian Church, which suffered significant damage to its exterior and interior in 1886. St. John's, next door, was relatively unharmed; St. Michael's Episcopal Church shared sanctuary space with the Lutherans while the old church was being repaired.

HAYNE STREET. In the 1830s city authorities made vigorous efforts to increase the city's commercial prospects. They looked to Hayne Street, named for Robert Y. Hayne, the famed senator of the Hayne–Webster debates and later mayor of Charleston, as a key to that development. Business owners constructed a number of buildings near the Charleston Hotel and business prospered. The earthquake of 1886 damaged several buildings sufficiently to force their demolition. The gap can be seen on the left side of the street.

ROPER HOSPITAL. After the 1886 earthquake, the wings of Roper Hospital at the corner of Queen and Mazyck (now Logan Street) were deemed unfit for use. The hospital sold the property, and the new owners retained the central section and adapted it into apartments and built homes on the site of the demolished wings. Known as the Marlborough Apartments, the central section stood until Hurricane Hugo in 1989, after which the owners demolished it.

MEDICAL COLLEGE OF SOUTH CAROLINA. Shown here with its appearance scarred by the 1886 earthquake is the Medical College, at the corner of Queen and Franklin Streets. Not only was the Medical College the sole institution of its type in the state, but it was also alone in the lower South. Frederick Wesner designed the school, which opened in 1824 with 7 professors and 50 students. Eventually, the college moved to quarters north of Calhoun Street, and the government demolished the building to develop Robert Mills Manor at the end of the Great Depression.

OLD HOSPITAL. "At the corner stood the building afterward known as the Trapman Street Hospital. . . . It was a long, low, wooden building, quite unbeautiful. . . . The old house is gone now; a cyclone wrecked its roof and an earthquake shook the chimneys down. . . . Nothing ever grew where the hospital stood; not a green leaf or blade of grass; not even vetch grew there, though vetch will grow almost anywhere." (John Bennett, "Trapman Street Hospital Tales—The Thirsty Dead," *The Doctor to the Dead*, 1943.)

LOWER KING STREET. This photograph shows lower King Street, including the Carolina Guards Armory, with damage from the 1911 hurricane. The storm was a surprise to many Charlestonians when it struck on Sunday, August 27. Winds of 106 miles per hour did substantial damage not only to the city, but also to the rice plantations south of the city. After the storm many planters elected to not repair their embankments and gave up rice planting, ending the grand epoch in South Carolina history. This photograph shows the section of King Street where the Library Society building was constructed three years later.

THE CHARLESTON LIBRARY SOCIETY. The Society constructed this beautiful Beaux Arts building at 164 King Street in 1914. Though the Society is the nation's third oldest subscription library, this was the first structure specifically designed for its use. The Library Society was organized in 1748 by a group of Charlestonians who desired to "save their descendants from sinking into savagery." The Library Society encouraged the founding of the College of Charleston and The Charleston Museum.

KING STREET. This 1883 view is substantially different from how the street appeared a century later. The City demolished all the buildings on the left for the Charleston Place project. The four-story building with the balustrade around the roof, on the right side of the street, was the Academy of Music. Originally built as a department store in 1852, the building was converted into a theatre in 1869 to replace the burned Charleston Theatre. A little past the Academy is another tall structure, the Victoria Hotel. This is where crew members of the *H.L. Hunley* lodged in 1863. Both the Academy of Music and the Victoria Hotel were torn down in the twentieth century; the Academy in 1936, the Victoria in 1970.

KING STREET. This photograph, capturing King Street at night in the middle of the twentieth century, appears to have been taken from the top of the Francis Marion Hotel at the corner of Calhoun and King Streets. By the end of the century only two businesses on the eastern side of King Street seen in this photograph were still in operation on the street: Croghan's Jewelry and The Keg.

KAHAL KADOSH BETH ELOHIM. The Lords Proprietors extended religious freedom not only to nearly all Christians (excluding Catholics), but to any sect recognizing a single deity. A Jewish community dated from the city's early days, though the community did not organize a synagogue until 1749. It was the second to be organized in British North America and is the oldest in continuous use. By 1790 Charleston had the largest Jewish population in the United States.

The present synagogue of Kahal Kadosh Beth Elohim at 90 Hasell Street replaced an earlier structure destroyed in the fire of 1835. The building is a Greek Revival jewel, constructed at the same time and with many of the same builders and craftsmen as the Charleston Hotel one block away.

In 1824 members of the congregation formed the Reformed Society of Israelites, which practiced a modernized form of service in the English language. With the rebuilding of the synagogue and the installation of an organ, many of the more conservative and orthodox members withdrew to form their own congregations. This synagogue is regarded as the first of the Reform sect in Judaism.

St. Mary's. The Carolina colony was notable for the religious toleration outlined in its first constitution. Early congregations of Quakers and Baptists existed near those of the Anglican Church and the French Huguenots. There was one notable exception, Roman Catholics. Deemed to be enemies of the Crown and English liberty, Catholics were forced to worship surreptitiously from the colony's founding in 1670 until after the Revolutionary War. Founded in 1789, St. Mary's, at 95 Hasell Street, is the mother church for all Roman Catholics in the Carolinas and Georgia. Constructed in 1838, the church is the third on the site. Many of the early members were refugees from Saint-Domingue, including the family of the Comte de Grasse, whose naval victory off the Virginia capes ensured Washington's later success at Yorktown. Two of de Grasse's daughters are buried in the churchyard.

TRINITY METHODIST CHURCH. Trinity Methodist Church is arguably the most beautiful of Charleston's temple-form churches. Architect E.C. Jones designed the church as the home of the Third Presbyterian Church, which was completed in 1850. Classical antecedents of the building include the Temple of Castor and Pollux in Rome.

MARKET HALL. This building, at the head of Charleston's historic market, is the design of architect E.B. White. It sits above the building originally designated as a meat market, thus explaining the rams' heads and bucrania in the frieze of the structure. A truly elegant structure, it was a meeting hall of the market's commissioners but has served other purposes in its long life. Confederate forces centralized their recruiting and resupply here during the Civil War. Since 1899 the United Daughters of the Confederacy have had a museum in the hall, although damage from Hurricane Hugo forced a renovation and the temporary transfer of the museum to other quarters.

THE CUSTOMS HOUSE. The story of the Customs House, located at 200 East Bay, is among the most interesting of any public building in Charleston. In 1847 after purchasing land at the foot of Market Street, the government announced a design competition for replacement of the Old Exchange. Several architects submitted designs, including one that may have resembled a castle, by Smithsonian architect James Renwick. Though local commissioners selected one design by E.C. Jones, in a classical fashion featuring a large dome, the final design was a combination of the more impressive portions of the various plans.

The design that the Treasury Department originally adopted called for a cruciform-shaped building crowned by an elaborate dome. The builders used New Jersey and New York granite for construction. Amni Burnham Young, a federally employed architect, drew the plans, but Charleston architect E.B. White supervised the project. Work began in 1849 and progressed sluggishly in the decade prior to the Civil War. The difficulty and expense of transporting stone from the Northeast and laying a firm foundation on Charleston's muddy waterfront contributed to delays as did the decaying political situation. The government cut appropriations to the project just before the Civil War began and work did not resume until 1867. The overall design was streamlined after the war due to political and economic factors. Architects truncated the northern and southern arms of the cruciform and did not build the dome. Still, it was not until 1879 that the building was completed.

The total cost of the building, originally estimated at $370,000, came to more than $3 million, requiring 19 separate acts of Congress. The Customs House is Charleston's largest stone building and contains one of the city's most inspiring interior spaces. Interestingly enough, less than 100 years after construction, the federal government seriously considered demolishing the building in the 1950s. Thankfully, local opinion and regard for the structure was sufficient to save the building.

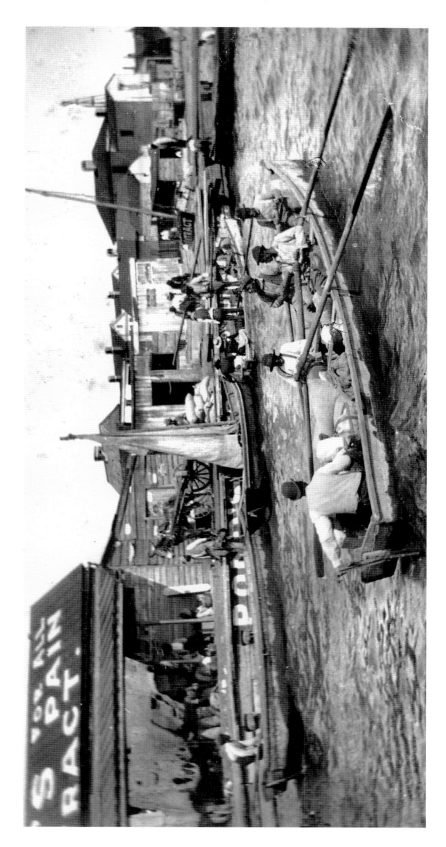

MOSQUITO FLEET. Perhaps no braver Charlestonians ever existed than those who took these tiny boats far beyond the coast to catch fish for the city's market. Descriptions of the fleet can be found as early as 1817, though it is believed that the fleet was in existence long before that date. Once again we turn to DuBose Heyward—this time to describe these intrepid sailors:

One by one the boats shoved off, and lay in the stream while they adjusted their spritsails and rigged their full jibs abeam, like spinnakers, for the free run to the sea. . . . Custom had reduced adventure to commonplace; yet it was inconceivable that men could put out, in the face of unsettled weather, for a point beyond sight of land, and exhibit no uneasiness or fear. Yet bursts of loud, loose laughter, and snatches of song blew back to the wharf long after the boats were in mid-stream.

The wind continued to come in sudden flaws, and once the little craft had gotten clear of the wharves, the fleet made swift but erratic progress. There were moments when they would seem to mark time upon the choppy waters of the bay; then suddenly a flaw would bear down on them, whipping the water as it came, and, filling the sails, would fairly lift the slender bows as it drove them forward. By the time that the leisurely old city was sitting down to its breakfast, the fleet had disappeared into the horizon. . . ." (DuBose Heyward, *Porgy*, 1925.)

A Charleston writer recorded this rowing chant about 1910: "Rosy am a han'some gal! / Haul away Rosy Haul away gal / Fancy slippers and fancy shawl! / Haul away Rosy, Haul-away / Rosy gwine ter de fancy ball! / Haul away Rosy Haul Haul away gal!"

73

WATERFRONT. Charleston's sleepy waterfront is seen in this early-twentieth-century photograph. In the center is the grand Customs House. On the left side of the photo is the wharf for the ferry to Mount Pleasant. To the right of the Customs House is the pier from which the fishermen of the "Mosquito Fleet" departed on their hazardous journeys to the great ocean deep. Two of the docks used by the Port Utilities Commission are on the right.

EAST BAY STREET. This c. 1897 view shows the city when electric streetcars first traveled Charleston's streets. Long called "The Bay," the street was the center of wholesale trade in Charleston, the counterpart to retail-oriented King Street. Warehouses, factors, and grocers' offices all were located along this thoroughfare.

WATERFRONT. "It was Porgy's custom, when the day's work was done and he had exchanged a part of his collections for his evening meal of fish and bread, to sit at his front window and watch the world pass by. The great cotton wharves lay up the river, beyond the row; and when the cotton season was on, he loved to sit in the dusk and see the drays go by. They would sweep into view with a loud thunder of wheels on the cobbles; and from his low seat they loomed huge and mysterious in the gathering dark. Sometimes there would be twenty of them in a row, with great swiftly stepping mules, crouched figures of drivers, and bales piled toweringly above them. Always Porgy experienced a vague and not unpleasant fear when the drays swung past. There was power, vast, awe inspiring; it could so easily crush him were he in its path. But here, safe within his window, he could watch it with perfect safety. At times when the train was unusually long, the sustained, rhythmic thunder and the sweep of form after form past his window produced an odd pleasurable detachment in his mind, and pictures of strange things and places would brighten and fade." (DuBose Heyward, *Porgy*, 1925.)

THE DOCKS FOR CLYDE LINE. For more than 60 years, the Clyde Line, later Clyde-Mallory, was a major presence on Charleston's waterfront. The first Clyde ship arrived in Charleston in 1886. The line's ships, named for American Indian tribes, conveyed passengers from New York and Boston to Charleston, and then to Jacksonville, along with shipments of cotton, naval stores, and lumber. Their dock was located on Vendue Range, where the entrance to Waterfront Park is today. The buildings burned in June 1955.

WATERFRONT. Here is Charleston's waterfront in the late nineteenth century, with workers "toating" the great staple product of the lower state. Rice continued to be grown on the plantations surrounding Charleston after the Civil War, though it never recovered its exalted place in the economy. Production grew from 15,337 tierces in 1866–1867 to 55,060 in 1879, and then a slow decline ensued. "Carolina Gold" was doomed when two successive hurricanes in 1910 and 1911 struck the South Carolina coast. Owners chose not to repair their heavily damaged dikes, and families began selling their plantations to Northern "winter residents," who used them as hunting preserves and winter homes. The last rice planter harvested his final crop in 1927.

THREE

FRENCH QUARTER

The name French Quarter is a modern term created to describe an area in the city's center encompassing the northern portion of the ancient walled city. The wall's northern line ran parallel to the present Market, where Cumberland Street runs today. The northeastern corner was located where the Customs House stands today. The wall ran south along East Bay to where the Missroon House stands today, where it turned west and ran parallel to Water Street, which was known as VanderHorst Creek. The western portion of the wall ran along Meeting Street.

The name of the district is derived from the influence of two distinct waves of French immigrants on the neighborhood. The first, coming soon after 1685, were the French Huguenots, forced by Louis XIV to leave Roman Catholic France because of their Protestant religion. Many settled in this area of town, but more importantly, they established their church in the center of the district, where it still stands today.

The subsequent wave of immigrants actually arrived here from French Saint-Domingue, in the Caribbean, as refugees from a slave rebellion there. Many in this second influx of settlers also found homes in the neighborhood. Most of the buildings in the area are of a later date, generally after 1796, when a devastating fire swept this portion of the city. However, the oldest public building in the city, the Powder Magazine, is on Cumberland Street, the northern boundary of the quarter.

STATE STREET. This is a view of State Street looking north, taken opposite from the corner of Chalmers Street. The handsome brick building in the center is a double tenement that George Locke constructed sometime after 1832. The three-story dwelling next door is one of the street's earlier houses, possibly dating to soon after the street was widened in 1813. The frame house, the corner of which is visible in the left of this picture, was moved to the corner of Chalmers and Meeting Streets in 1973.

St. Philip's Episcopal Church. This is the third St. Philip's Episcopal Church, the oldest congregation in the city, founded in 1680. The first church stood at the intersection of Meeting and Broad Streets, where St. Michael's stands today. The second church was built at this location at 146 Church Street beginning in 1711. The church pictured here dates from 1835, the year a fire burned the earlier structure. The location of the church at the edge of the walled city had great significance to the townspeople. St. Philip's stands at the highest point in the old walled city. It sits at what was then the head of the central north-south street in the city. The church was built to project into the street so prominently that traffic was routed through the western portico of the building. The spire was the tallest in the city until the completion of St. Michael's in 1761. When completed the church not only was regarded as the most handsome structure in the city, but it created a compelling vista for the townspeople. Besides being aesthetically pleasing, the church was an indisputable reminder of the prominence and majesty of the King's church in the Carolina colony.

When this church, shown in the photograph on the opposite page, was built following a tragic fire in 1835, the congregation wished that the original building be replicated as exactly as possible. Architect Robert Mills, who at the time was employed by the federal government in Washington, D.C., was asked by the congregation to draw the reconstruction plans. Mills admired the old church and commented favorably on it in his *Statistics of South Carolina*. He made repairs to the church in the 1820s and was very familiar with the earlier structure, apparently creating a series of architectural drawings used during subsequent repairs. Working in Charleston during the summer of 1835, Mills gave the church plans that allowed them to rebuild a nearly identical successor.

After the church burned, the city council requested that the vestry rebuild the church in a way so that Church Street could be straightened. This would have involved laying foundations 48 feet east of those of the original church. This, the vestry refused to do, in part stating that the ground was not stable enough in the area to support the building. The conflicting parties agreed to a compromise of 24 feet, an agreement that preserved the remarkable vista seen in this photograph. The 1838 building was not constructed with a steeple. Architect E.B. White designed a much different spire than the original steeple when he was asked to add a tower ten years later in 1848. Fortunately, White's expert handling of proportions and Classical-revival style resulted in a most elegant steeple, a fitting ornament for Mills's graceful reconstruction of the earlier church.

St. Philip's Episcopal Church. The "Great Shock" of 1886 severely damaged St. Philip's, destroying its western portico, a substantial portion of the steeple, and causing large cracks throughout the building.

St. Philip's Church. When the second St. Philip's Church burned in 1835, parishioners were united to rebuild the exterior exactly as before. They decided, however, to change the interior substantially. The earlier church had large piers supporting the balconies, which while fondly remembered by the congregants, were not so well loved as to be replaced. The interior instead was modeled on that of St. Martin-in-the-Fields in London, with elegant Corinthian columns, plaster-ornamented arches, and a general exuberance very different from the colonial-era building.

HUGUENOT CHURCH. A local historian once said that the Huguenot Church was "nothing but a tent, but a fine tent." When the congregation constructed this building at 136 Church Street in 1845, it was the city's first Gothic Revival building of worship, a style previously used for smaller structures. The congregation of French Huguenots dates to a period soon after Louis XIV's Revocation of the Edict of Nantes in 1685. This is the third structure to house the congregation. Plaques inside honor the many distinguished Americans of Huguenot ancestry.

THE OLD POWDER MAGAZINE. Located at 21 Cumberland Street, the Old Powder Magazine is the only public building standing in the city that dates from the rule of the Lords Proprietors. The Proprietors were eight English noblemen who had supported the restoration of the English monarchy after the rule of Oliver Cromwell. As a reward for their service, King Charles II granted them the colony of Carolina. The purpose of the Old Powder Magazine, built about 1713, was to house the colony's supply of gunpowder. Serving variously as a magazine, print shop, and even a wine cellar for the Manigault family, the building survived to be rescued by the Colonial Dames in 1902. This was the first historic building in Charleston to be saved from demolition and preserved as a landmark.

THE LITTLE ITALY INN. This handsome building once stood at the corner of Cumberland and State Streets. The site is now a parking lot.

84

STATE STREET. State Street and vicinity were long a center of Charleston's auction markets. Shortly before the Civil War a city ordinance restricted slave sales to this area. Auctioneers continued to locate themselves there into the early decades of the twentieth century. The large frame building in the center of the photograph housed the business of auctioneer Arthur P. Cohen. State Street was first known as Union Street, a commemoration of the joining of the English and Scottish crowns in 1707. The name was changed in 1812 to the more appropriate American-sounding name in the first year of the second war with Great Britain.

QUEEN STREET. This photo was taken about 1930 on the first block of Queen Street. Barber William Neal occupied 15 Queen, and next door was the Sanitary Lunchroom, identified by the Coca-Cola sign.

RYAN'S AUCTION MART. Though slavery was the central feature of Charleston's antebellum economy, the auctions that took place along the city's waterfront caused no small amount of embarrassment to residents. Visitors would write of the odious nature of the sales, with auctioneers calling out the specific attributes of slaves while potential buyers examined them for defects.

Sales for the most part took place on the north side of the Old Exchange Building, which served as the post office in that era. The City attempted to move sales off the waterfront, but lax enforcement meant that the change never took place. In 1856 the City passed an ordinance that required auctions to move indoors, and auctioneers established several "offices" in the area of Chalmers, Queen, and State Streets.

This photograph shows 6 Chalmers Street, the only building in the city that can be documented as an auction house for slaves. Known as Ryan's Auction Mart, the structure had a large gold star placed on the arch with the a gilt inscription "MART." For many years, from the 1920s until Hurricane Hugo, the building served as a museum of slavery in the Carolina Lowcountry.

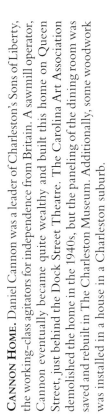

THE PINK HOUSE. Located at number 17 Chalmers, the Pink House is a familiar Charleston landmark, long a favorite subject of photographers and artists attempting to capture the city's unique charm. The date of construction for the building is usually placed in the second decade of the eighteenth century, making it one of Charleston's oldest structures. A tavern-keeper owned the house by 1750, as this area was known as Charleston's bawdy district during the colonial era. One wonders whether photographers know the original occupation of this grande dame.

CANNON HOME. Daniel Cannon was a leader of Charleston's Sons of Liberty, the working-class agitators for independence from Britain. A sawmill operator, Cannon eventually became quite wealthy and built this home on Queen Street, just behind the Dock Street Theatre. The Carolina Art Association demolished the home in the 1940s, but the paneling of the dining room was saved and rebuilt in The Charleston Museum. Additionally, some woodwork was installed in a house in a Charleston suburb.

88

STATE STREET. Charles LePrince's automotive repair shop stood at 36 State Street when Albert Simons took this photograph. A young businessman rented the second floor of the building in 1938 for $35 a month. The stately three-story house next door was built about 1816.

Farther up the street can be seen the house that Robert N.S. and Paty Whitelaw later purchased. Mr. and Mrs. Whitelaw were among the city's most important cultural leaders in the twentieth century and a major force for preservation. As director of the Gibbes Art Gallery, he effectively inaugurated the institution's modern era. Not only did Whitelaw spearhead the project that resulted in *This is Charleston*, the first city-wide architectural survey undertaken in the nation, but he also was one of the founders of the Historic Charleston Foundation. His wife, Patti, was equally influential, particularly within the preservation community.

The Whitelaws purchased the residence at 42 State when it was at its nadir. Pigeons were roosting in the attic and access to the second floor came via a ladder. They used their own expertise and salvaged remnants of demolished homes to create one of Charleston's showplaces.

CHALMERS STREET. Charleston's most famous cobblestone street, Chalmers Street is the subject of this Albert Simons photograph. Hibernian Hall can be seen in the distance at the end of the street. The three-story brick dwelling, owned by the McInnes family for generations, is still standing. However, the stepped-gable auto shop and the handsome two-story stucco home have both given way to progress. A parking lot, enclosed by a brick wall patterned after the one found in Washington Park, is on the site.

OUTBUILDING FOR THE DANIEL CANNON HOUSE. This charming structure, with its eccentric roof line, is the outbuilding of the Daniel Cannon House at 45 Queen Street. It was originally constructed to serve a double tenement, explaining the building's two doors. When the Daniel Cannon House was demolished in the 1940s, the outbuilding was restored and turned into a private residence.

DILAPIDATED HOMES ON QUEEN STREET. Albert Simons captured forever the city's decaying conditions about 1930 with his photograph of these homes at 22–28 Queen Street. The Johnson family of Charleston built the townhouses in the last decade of the eighteenth century.

THE CORNER OF STATE STREET AND UNITY ALLEY. The intersection no longer resembles this photograph due to some substantial changes after 1900. The gable roof on the two-story brick dwelling, 18 State Street, was changed to a flat roof, similar to that found on Greek Revival–era dwellings. The stately three-story stucco dwelling with the "provisions" sign was torn down, which allowed the owners of 18 State to add a two-story piazza. Number 20 State Street, a portion of which is seen on the left side of the image, has remained essentially unchanged except for the painted sign between the first and second floors. It was this building that enabled identification of this photograph.

VIGILANT FIRE INSURANCE COMPANY. Charleston enthusiast John Bennett took this photograph of the Vigilant Fire Insurance Company Building at 41 State Street.

UNKNOWN STREET SCENE. The location of this photograph cannot be determined, though it has characteristics that place it in the city's waterfront area, perhaps in the French Quarter. Note the hogsheads, the spools for wire or rope, and what looks like an old gun carriage.

QUEEN STREET. Daniel Cruikshank built numbers 18 and 20 Queen Street, seen here in the center of this turn–of-the-century photograph, soon after the fire of 1796. Cruikshank was a tanner who practiced his trade on the premises; the presence of large amounts of salt residue, used to treat hides, was found during a restoration in the 1950s.

The two-story structure located to the left of Mr. Cruikshank's houses was built as a cotton warehouse in 1830. The Footlight Players, a local theatrical group, now use it as a theatre.

PLANTERS INN. Here is another famous landmark, pictured just before its modern restoration. The Planters Inn, located at 135 Church Street, was one of the preferred places to lodge when it was built in 1809. Smaller hotels like the Planters Inn suffered with the advent of larger establishments such as the Charleston Hotel and the Mills House.

By the beginning of the twentieth century, the Planters Inn, like many other hotels in the city, was better known for the services it could provide than for the quality of the lodging. At the time of this photograph (at left), it was no longer a hotel, but was used for storage.

The interior photograph above was taken shortly before the inn's restoration in the 1930s. The Works Progress Administration restored and converted the hotel into a theatre. The head of the federal program, Harry Hopkins, took a special interest in the theatre and considered it to be one of the flagship projects of the Depression-era relief agency. The WPA installed interior wood and plasterwork from the demolished Radcliffe-King House at the corner of Meeting and George Streets in the public rooms, while gutting a substantial portion of the building to create the actual theatre space. The Planters Inn stands on the location of the first building to be constructed as a theatre in America, also known as the Dock Street Theatre, the name adopted for the new facility.

F O U R

ANSONBOROUGH

The "suburbs" of Charleston in the eighteenth and nineteenth centuries were those areas outside of the original walled city and above Broad Street. The city's original plan called for its streets to run at right angles in a grid-like pattern. However, as the city grew, long before the rise of planning boards, individuals developed their own tracts of land without government oversight. In defense of these early developers, the dysfunctional nature of the city's early street planning can be explained by natural impediments that forced separation between the city's parts. Creeks and other bodies of water often formed a part of a development's boundary.

Ansonborough is regarded as Charleston's first suburb, laid out by a distinguished British naval hero, Lord George Anson. Among his more famous exploits was the capture of the treasure-laden *Manila Galleon*. His early career was spent in Charleston and legend states he won this tract of land in a card game. Anson named the streets for himself, George and Anson, and for his ships, *Centurion*, *Scarborough*, and *Squirrel*. Regrettably, the latter three streets were renamed later. The southern boundary of Ansonborough is the

Market, which stands on a creek bed not filled in until about 1800. Thus, neither Church nor State Streets, both part of the town's original plan, run directly through to the streets of the suburb. Instead, Anson intersects with Market midway between the two streets. Many of the homes in Ansonborough date from the late 1830s and 1840s. In 1838 a monstrous fire burned most of the area from the waterfront to King Street. Considered one of the city's most fashionable areas, modern-day Ansonborough not only encompasses the naval officer's land, but also three other historic sections.

BURGES POOL. Few cities are adaptive as Charleston. Passersby would probably not realize that behind the austere facade of the Middleton-Pinckney House, now headquarters of the Spoleto Festival, was the city's municipal swimming facility. The pool was named in honor of George D. Burges, a Charleston swimmer, whose aviation heroics garnered him fame during World War II. Burges was a graduate of the College of Charleston and competed in a number of long-distance swimming contests. A small alley, running alongside number 14 George Street, still carries his name.

WILLIAM RHETT HOUSE. Rhett, a sometimes–rebellious colonial officer, built the dwelling about 1714 at 54 Hasell Street, and some consider it to be the oldest house in the city. In 1718 he captured Stede Bonnet, the last of the pirates to menace the city's shores.

Confederate General Wade Hampton was born in the house in 1818. By the time of this photograph, locals regarded the residence as a house of assignation. In 1941 the owners of Dean Hall and Cypress Gardens, Mr. and Mrs. Benjamin Kittredge, purchased the home and completely restored it.

293 EAST BAY. This is the residence of Nathaniel Heyward, the pre-eminent rice planter of antebellum Charleston who spent time overseas in the European Lowcountries studying diking systems. Using the same principles here, he was able to manipulate the tidal flow of rivers south of Charleston to grow immense quantities of rice. Many of his plantations were named for towns he visited including Rotterdam, Copenhagen, and Hamburg.

64 HASELL STREET. The structure on the right of this picture suffered significant damage in the earthquake. In addition to the collapsed piazza, shown here, the house was badly cracked in some places. Total damage was estimated to be $2,050. The structure with columns on the left, the Palmetto Guard Armory, was only lightly affected, with damage coming to $250.

BENNETT'S RICE MILL. Governor Thomas Bennett built this grand structure in 1844 as a rice mill. The mill survived the end of the rice epoch and a variety of uses until the City condemned it as hazardous in the 1950s. The Preservation Society intervened and made plans to restore it. However, before work could begin, nature intervened and a tornado laid waste to it. Afterwards, the City demolished all but one side of the building. The ruin stands in the middle of a parking lot used by the South Carolina State Ports Authority, still gazing out over the Cooper River.

55 LAURENS STREET. This vine-covered house was built late in the Adamesque period, about 1818. Much larger than most homes in the neighborhood, it was restored and converted into condominiums in the 1980s.

ZION PRESBYTERIAN CHURCH. Charleston suffered a great blow to its history when it lost Zion Presbyterian Church on Calhoun Street in 1959. Zion was built between 1858 and 1859 to serve as the Presbyterian congregation for slaves in the city. As the congregation grew, so did the number of white members, which included the building's architect, E.C. Jones, who was an elder of the church. Jones designed the floor plan so that all congregants, black and white, were seated on the same level, similar to Calvary Episcopal Church on Beaufain Street.

FIVE

HARLESTON VILLAGE

Harleston Village has its roots in the earliest settlement of South Carolina. John Coming, first mate on the ship Carolina, the first ship to land settlers here, received a grant for the land in this area of town. His wife, Affra Harleston Coming, survived him and left a portion of the tract to the Anglican Church in the colony as glebe land (land owned by a parish church for revenue). The remainder was left to her nephew in England, John Harleston. The village was planned in 1770, with street names honoring prominent provincial and imperial politicians of the time: Pitt, Smith, Bull, Montagu, Wentworth, Barre, Beaufain, Rutledge, Lynch (now changed to Ashley), and Gadsden. This section of the book includes the Glebe Lands, connected to the village through

Mrs. Coming. Additionally, the College of Charleston is located here, since the college's first classes were held in St. Philip's rectory on Glebe Street, before the Revolutionary-era barracks were converted a few years later in the area only a block north.

60 MONTAGU STREET. Once this house had a beautiful vista of broad marshland and the Ashley River, due to its location near the western end of Montagu Street, at number 60. Theodore Gaillard built the house about 1800, and its later owners included a Revolutionary War general, a British consul, and a member of the famed Bennett family of Charleston. This last gentleman, Washington Jefferson Bennett, entertained Robert E. Lee when he made his only visit to Charleston following the Civil War.

WESTERNMOST BLOCK OF MONTAGU STREET. Jonathan Steinmeyer, a sawmill operator, built the first house on the right, number 62 Meeting Street, in 1854. Like its neighbor at 60 Montagu, it once had a superlative view across the marshes to the Ashley River.

The dwelling at number 64, which is partially visible in the photograph, is another Bennett family house, built by the senior Thomas Bennett in the first decade of the nineteenth century.

89 BEAUFAIN STREET. This photograph shows the home of United States and Confederate States Navy officer Duncan Ingraham. Commodore Ingraham became a national hero in 1853 when he defied Austria and demanded the release of an American citizen held onboard one of her ships. For this, Congress awarded him a gold medal. At the beginning of the Civil War, Ingraham returned to his native state to command all Confederate naval forces in South Carolina. Ingraham entertained Robert E. Lee, a longtime friend, in the house when Lee commanded military forces in South Carolina, Georgia, and Florida early in the conflict.

108 BEAUFAIN STREET. This residence was the home of James Butler Campbell, who sued to keep a factory from being built on the public land around Colonial Lake. The dwelling was built sometime after 1842, when Governor Thomas Bennett purchased the lot. He willed the house to two of his maiden granddaughters, who were children of James Butler Campbell. At the death of the last granddaughter, the house was willed to the Presbyterian Church to establish the Argyle-Louden Memorial Home. It was meant to provide a refuge for Presbyterian and Huguenot women of "gentle birth and small means." The house was used as a rest home until 1971.

87 AND 89 WENTWORTH STREET. Built prior to the Revolutionary War, these connected homes form an interesting contrast, as they were constructed at the same time. The home to the left, number 87, was significantly altered in the nineteenth century, with the addition of a full third story, while number 89 remains a relatively intact colonial dwelling house. The homes stand on the glebe land once owned by St. Philip's Episcopal Church. The frame structure (right foreground) was built in the late nineteenth century.

COLONIAL LAKE. Few cities of Charleston's size can boast of such substantial parks. The city is encompassed on all sides by public spaces including the Battery, Waterfront Park, Hampton Park, and Colonial Lake. The latter park, shown in this late-nineteenth-century photograph, actually is the oldest of all.

Designated by the colonial-era legislature as "a Common for Charles Towne," the space centered on a large body of water known even today as "The Pond." As the city developed, some citizens forgot the public nature of the land and built homes upon it. A tract of land to the west of the lake proved to be the final straw for an attorney, James Butler Campbell, who lived in a residence facing the lake. He sued the City to keep a sash and blind factory from being built on the site, arguing that the land had been set aside to allow for public space. He added that the land was also reserved to keep open the western side of the peninsula for the western and southerly breezes that cooled and aerated the city. This argument won the day, and the City officially dedicated the park on the anniversary of its centennial in 1883.

103

CALVARY EPISCOPAL CHURCH. Another of E.B. White's churches, Calvary Episcopal was unique because it was the first to be established in the city for slaves after the Denmark Vesey plot of 1822. Very specific arrangements were made within the church for the slave congregation and the whites that attended to oversee the services. Blacks entered the church through one door, whites through another. White congregants used slightly raised white pews, while slaves used brown-painted pews.

Despite these arrangements, there was public outcry when the church was established in 1847. Many feared that it might serve as another seedbed of rebellion. James L. Petigru and other racial moderates calmed fears, and the church proved to be very successful. In 1940 this building at the corner of Beaufain and Wilson Streets was sold to the Housing Authority, and the congregation moved to Line Street. The original church was demolished in 1961.

149 WENTWORTH STREET. With 13,883 square feet, the residence of Francis Silas Rodgers was one of the most imposing homes built in Charleston during the post–Civil War era. This photograph shows the house during World War II when the Coast Guard had its headquarters in the building.

CHARLESTON'S RED CROSS. Shown here are the officers and staff of the local Red Cross when their headquarters were located at 144 Wentworth. Miss Mary Jane Ross, resident of number 1 Meeting Street, allowed the organization to use her mother's house on Wentworth Street during World War I. When Miss Ross passed away, she left the home to be used by non-sectarian, non-political organizations, a usage that continued for many years.

Shown in this photo are the following: (first row) Miss Mary Hard, Mrs. Manning Simmons, Mrs. Frank Barron, Mrs. Ashley Halsey, Miss Frances K. Mazyck, and Mrs. Christopher G. Horre; (second row) Dr. Kenneth Lynch, Mrs. I.G. Ball, Miss Rebecca Bryan, Mr. W. King McDowell, Mrs. I.K. Heyward, Mrs. John Bennett, and Mr. J.T. Coleman.

BAKER HOSPITAL. Charleston physicians Archibald Baker Sr. and Lawrence Craig constructed Baker Hospital at number 55 Ashley Avenue in 1912. It is an amalgam of Italian Renaissance and Mission styles. Several generations of Charlestonians could proudly state they were born in the tall hospital that faced Colonial Lake, before it was converted into condominiums.

DAWSON RESIDENCE. This post-earthquake photograph is of Francis Warrington Dawson's dwelling on Bull Street. Should anyone ever wish to make a movie about a fascinating Charlestonian, Dawson would be a worthy subject. An Englishman who sympathized with the South, Dawson changed his birth name and signed onboard a blockade runner destined for North Carolina. After reaching the South, he enlisted in Lee's army and participated in more than a dozen battles before being captured and imprisoned. The end of the conflict found him in Richmond, where he wrote for a newspaper until it failed. A friend there suggested that he go to Charleston.

After a year here, he purchased the *Charleston News*, which later combined with the venerable *Charleston Courier*. The combined company is the ancestor of today's *Post & Courier*. Dawson's individual and outspoken editorial style made many friends, and nearly as many enemies, but it enabled him to exert power on the city's and state's affairs as no other editor before or since. He is credited with coining the phrase "bring the mills to the cotton," and he encouraged the establishment of a vigorous textile industry in the state. He also carried on a longtime campaign against dueling, for which he was knighted by the Pope. Ironically, he was murdered by a man whom he rightly suspected of being involved with a French domestic servant employed in his household.

CONFEDERATE VETERANS' AUDITORIUM. John Thomson, a seed store merchant on King Street, left a portion of his estate to fund the straightening of King Street. Instead, the money was used to construct this auditorium on Rutledge Avenue in 1898 to accommodate the Confederate veterans' reunion the following year. Architect Frank Milburn of Charlotte, who also was responsible for completing the Statehouse in Columbia, was retained to design the structure. Contractors had just over four months to complete work or risk a fine for each day of delay. Literally working day and night (an electrical plant was installed for artificial lighting), contractors finished Thomson Auditorium three days before the deadline and just two weeks before the reunion began. This photograph shows the building decorated for the event.

Veterans from all over the South attended, with railways including the Louisville & Nashville putting ticket prices at 1¢ a mile. South Carolina veterans were asked as gracious hosts to share their blankets with old soldiers visiting from their sister Southern states. The auditorium stood on Rutledge Avenue just south of its intersection with Calhoun Street. In 1907 the auditorium became the home of The Charleston Museum. In 1981, shortly after the museum moved to a new building on Meeting Street, the auditorium burned to the ground. Only the columns of the front portico were salvaged. They stand on the edge of present-day Cannon Park.

THE ISAAC JENKINS MIKELL HOUSE. Located at 94 Rutledge, this ornate residence represents the high tide of antebellum affluence in coastal South Carolina. In 1853, a Sea Island cotton planter built the home, which combines elements of the earlier Greek Revival style with the Italianate style that was then the rage. A contemporary description of the residence said it was one of the city's "most ambitious private dwellings." One distinguishing feature is the use of rams' heads to form the capitals of the columns. From 1930 until 1960, the residence served as Charleston's first public library.

WILLIAM BLACKLOCK HOUSE. Yet another Adamesque jewel in Charleston's crown, the William Blacklock house is a designated National Historic Landmark. Built around 1800, the house, number 18 Bull Street, conforms to the alternate house plan popular in the city in that era—the double house. With two rooms fronting the street and four rooms per floor, it was a more spacious plan for city dwelling, compared to the more popular single-house form. This house has some of the most beautiful and refined brickwork in the city.

William Blacklock was a wealthy wine merchant in post-Revolutionary Charleston, dealing in Madeira wines so admired in the city. He served on the commission responsible for building City Hall, along with amateur architect Gabriel Manigault. Stylistic similarities have caused architectural historians to conjecture that Manigault was also responsible for this home.

109

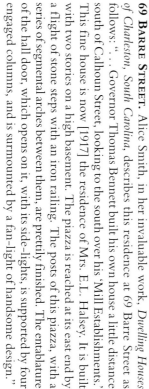

69 BARRE STREET. Alice Smith, in her invaluable work, *Dwelling Houses of Charleston, South Carolina*, describes this residence at 69 Barre Street as follows: ". . . Governor Thomas Bennett built his own house a little distance south of Calhoun Street, looking to the south over his 'Mill Establishments.' This fine house is now [1917] the residence of Mrs. E.L. Halsey. It is built with two stories on a high basement. The piazza is reached at its east end by a flight of stone steps with an iron railing. The posts of this piazza, with a series of segmental arches between them, are prettily finished. The entablature of the hall door, which opens on it, with its side-lights, is supported by four engaged columns, and is surmounted by a fan-light of handsome design."

MEMMINGER SCHOOL. Late-antebellum architect E.C. Jones designed Memminger School, which served the city as the primary educational facility for women into the twentieth century. It was named in honor of Christopher Gustavus Memminger, an orphaned German immigrant who rose to become the Confederacy's first secretary of the treasury. Memminger was an ardent advocate of public schools and served on the board of commissioners for Charleston's free schools. Originally known as Girl's High and Normal School, it had the added responsibility of training young women to teach in the state's schools. The school stood at number 4 St. Philip's Street before it was demolished and replaced with an International-style building.

DOORWAY AT 11 MONTAGU STREET. Mrs. Elizabeth Schmidt and Robert Eason Conner constructed this residence over a period of 11 years. A truly lovely home, the dwelling has one of the most beautiful "piazza screens" in the city, shown here.

Often called a "false front door" by visitors to the city, the piazza screen plays a crucial role in the livability of the single house. Most early single houses were originally constructed without side porches, known locally as "piazzas." The necessity of privacy required the development of a device to shield the dwelling's inhabitants from the street. As time passed, this screen began to serve as the residential "front door," often acquiring a more elaborate architectural treatment than the entrance door.

20 MONTAGU STREET. A riot of wisteria disguises the beautiful home that Daniel Cobia built at 20 Montagu Street. Several members of the Cobia family resided nearby in Harleston Village. Later owners included Dr. James Moultrie and Edward McCrady, a noted nineteenth-century South Carolina historian.

COLLEGE OF CHARLESTON. America's first municipal college, the College of Charleston had its nativity in this house at 6 Glebe Street in 1785. The house was constructed as the rectory for St. Philip's Church about 1770 on a tract of 17 acres left to the church by a parishioner, Robert Smith, rector of St. Philip's and a notable Revolutionary patriot, was named first president of the college in 1785. In 1795 he was consecrated first Episcopal bishop of South Carolina. Though of English birth, Smith served as chaplain to American forces during the struggle for independence until the British exiled him to St. Augustine after the city's capture in 1780. Appropriately, the house once again became the residence of the college's president, when descendants of Bishop Smith raised money to purchase and donate the house to the school in 1962.

RANDOLPH HALL. The main building of the College of Charleston is Randolph Hall, seen here set far back from George Street. This structure, built about 1820, replaced a "mass of ill looking and inconvenient buildings" that served the college in the early nineteenth century. William Strickland, an architect from Philadelphia, designed the central portion of the building. In 1850 Charleston architect E.B. White added the wings to the east and west sides and the refined Ionic portico seen in this photo. The grassy mound in the foreground is the school's old water source, the Cistern, where graduation is held each May.

The building is named in honor of Harrison Randolph, president of the college from 1897 to 1942. During his tenure he oversaw the modernization of the institution, expansion of library facilities, and enrollment of the first coeds in 1918.

SIX

EAST SIDE

Charleston's East Side is an area bounded on the south by Calhoun Street, east by the Cooper River, west by King Street, and north by the Cooper River Bridges. It includes the historic suburbs of Mazyckborough, Wraggsborough, and Hampstead.

Hampstead is the most northerly and the oldest of the suburbs in the neighborhood. Henry Laurens and some business associates developed it in 1769. They named the tract for a fashionable suburb located on a hill just outside of London. They named the streets as a political statement representing their Whig sentiments: Nassau, Hanover, Drake, Amherst, Hampden, America, Columbus, and Wolfe.

Alexander Mazyck laid out Mazyckborough shortly after the Revolution, and it is often hyphenated with the suburb to its immediate north, Wraggsborough. The builder named one street for himself, one for a female member of his family, and one for the nation's first president. Wraggsborough's streets are a family reunion, named for children who inherited the land: John, Judith, Henrietta, Mary, Ann, and Elizabeth.

Chapel Street represents the small church built in the center of the development.

In the first half of the nineteenth century, the East Side was one of Charleston's most fashionable neighborhoods and the center of much early industrial development. Due to its location outside the city limits (the City annexed the area in 1849), it was the home to many of Charleston's black residents, both slave and free, who wished to live unhindered by the lower city's strict racial laws.

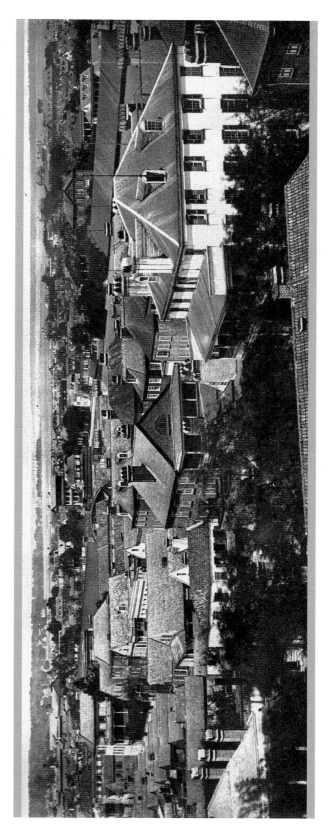

VIEW OF CHARLESTON'S EAST SIDE. This fascinating photograph was taken from the cupola of the Orphan House between 1865 (as it appears to have been taken by a Union photographer) and 1867 (when construction of St. Matthew's Lutheran Church began). St. Matthew's was built on the lots immediately across King Street from the Old Citadel. The dominating feature is the general elegance and refinement of the homes in this section of the city. Unfortunately the late nineteenth and the majority of the twentieth century would not be so kind to what were then known as the "upper wards of

353 MEETING STREET. Bennett's Pontiac is visible at the corner of Meeting and John Streets, across from where The Charleston Museum stands today.

THREE SISTERS. Charleston's "Three Sisters" sat near the corner of East Bay and Calhoun Streets, offering a well-bred welcome to generations of visitors and returning residents. Sadly, they were lost forever when they were torn down between 1962 and 1964.

THE OLD CITADEL. Built originally as an arsenal and guardhouse in the upper part of the city, the Old Citadel became the site of South Carolina's military school in 1842. A number of officers from the school served the Confederate cause during the Civil War. The building faces Marion Square, which was commonly known as Citadel Green.

A painting of the *Oath of the Horatii* by the famed French artist David supposedly was the inspiration for the building's interior. The school remained in this location until 1922, when it moved to a location on the Ashley River by Hampton Park.

20 CHARLOTTE STREET. Imagine being given a house for a wedding present. Now imagine if it were this superb antebellum residence. A wonderful example of the late Greek Revival period, this home at 20 Charlotte Street was the gift of Robert Martin to his daughter Ellen and her new husband, Joseph Daniel Aiken. The Aikens built the house between 1848 and 1849 and furnished it on a grand tour–honeymoon–buying trip while construction proceeded on it. Family tradition asserts that Aiken, who was responsible for much of the house's artwork, may have been the home's architect. His grandson, Albert Simons, was the architect whose photos appeared previously in the French Quarter chapter.

631 EAST BAY STREET. This stately Palladian villa is yet another piece of former waterfront property in Charleston. Henry Faber built it about 1837, and it was later home to John Joshua Ward of Waccamaw Neck near Georgetown, one of the state's wealthiest rice planters in 1860. So famous was the product of his plantations, that "Ward's big-grain yellow rice," Carolina Gold, was a familiar and favored commodity abroad. The English were especially appreciative of it. A recently deceased Charlestonian recalls walking into a London grocery in the 1930s to ask for a pound of their "very best rice." The clerk replied that they no longer had the very best rice, as Carolina rice had not been exported in a number of years.

36 CHARLOTTE STREET. The inscription on the back of this photograph reads as follows: "Mrs. Emma Julia Smith Whilden, daughter of Thomas P. Smith, in her 'Widow Weeds', shows northern 'Pay Visitors', how a Charlestonian pays a visit in the early days. 'Tinkle the bell', at the side front gate, the butler comes to the gate to take your card, before you are received. This picture taken at 36 Charlotte Street, and also show[s] the 'heirloom butler' Stewart. Four generations of his family have served the Smiths."

COURTENAY SCHOOL. Erected in 1889 at number 382 Meeting Street, the school honors one of the finest mayors Charleston has ever had. William Ashmead Courtenay, a veteran of the Confederate army, was elected in 1879, not a propitious time in the history of the city. However, during his 12-year term he modernized the city's services, established parks and public grounds, and led the city through two of the most serious crises that Charleston has ever faced—the cyclone of 1885 and the earthquake of 1886. This structure and five houses that ran parallel to it on Wragg Mall were razed in the 1940s to erect the current building.

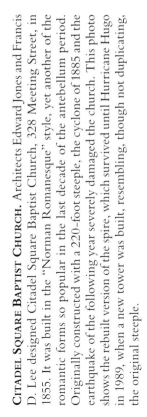

GARDEN TEMPLE ON ASHMEAD PLACE. Few buildings excel Gabriel Manigault's garden temple in classical elegance. However, this structure on Ashmead Place was not the main entrance to the dwelling; a door on the northern facade, facing John Street, served that purpose. While it is hard to imagine, this graceful little structure served as a tool storage facility for a gas station at the corner of Ashmead and Meeting Streets in the 1930s. The gas station is visible on the left.

CITADEL SQUARE BAPTIST CHURCH. Architects Edward Jones and Francis D. Lee designed Citadel Square Baptist Church, 328 Meeting Street, in 1855. It was built in the "Norman Romanesque" style, yet another of the romantic forms so popular in the last decade of the antebellum period. Originally constructed with a 220-foot steeple, the cyclone of 1885 and the earthquake of the following year severely damaged the church. This photo shows the rebuilt version of the spire, which survived until Hurricane Hugo in 1989, when a new tower was built, resembling, though not duplicating, the original steeple.

119

340 MEETING STREET. Charleston is renowned for its architectural variety and is recognized as having a nationally significant number of Georgian, Federal (called Adamesque locally for obvious reasons), Greek Revival, and Romantic Revival styles. However, there are but a handful of buildings from the Regency period, a fact due not so much to taste, but to economy. The primary architect to work in the city during the Regency period was William Jay, a native of Bath, England. Jay went first to Savannah, where his sister lived. There he designed a number of structures, including several private homes. Moving on to Charleston about 1819, he is credited with several homes, including the one pictured here, known to contemporaries as "Weyman's Folly," for its first owner Joseph T. Weyman. Over the years, this residence has passed through many hands, serving variously as a home, later as a hotel for the Salvation Army, and for private concerns. Finally, the federal government purchased it and used it as Shore Patrol Headquarters in World War II. The government demolished it in 1948 and constructed a federal office building.

COOPER RIVER BRIDGE. When the Cooper River Bridge opened in August 1929, it cost $5.75 million to build and was the longest bridge of its type in the world. The change it wrought on the city of Charleston and the surrounding region was immense, for it linked the city with the most direct route to Florida from the Northeast. Tourists began to flow into Charleston, although the real flood would occur after World War II. Additionally, it connected the old peninsular city with Mount Pleasant, which had once seemed very remote. Thereafter the city expanded north and south across the Ashley, surging out from the narrow strip of land where it had developed for 250 years.

121

VanderHorst Residence. In 1832 Elias VanderHorst built this Greek Revival dwelling house at the corner of Chapel and Alexander Streets in the suburb of Wraggsborough, located just north of the city limits. His family was one of the most prominent in the city, owning a substantial portion of Kiawah Island, wharf property, and a number of plantations. Colonel Arnoldus VanderHorst, his father, was intendant (mayor) when Washington visited in 1791 and was later governor of the state. Elias VanderHorst's wife, Ann Elliott Morris, was a member of the famed Morris family of New York and New Jersey.

SEVEN

WEST SIDE

The western side of the peninsula consists of several smaller suburbs including the Wragg Lands, Radcliffborough, the Elliott Lands, Cannonborough, Rugely Lands, and Elliottborough. Much like the East Side, this was a diverse neighborhood, with a number of industrial facilities such as saw and rice mills, and the homes of many of Charleston's black community. Large sections of the present West Side were marsh and ponds, not filled in until the late nineteenth and early twentieth centuries.

6 THOMAS STREET. A large magnolia shades the front of the home of Robert Barnwell Rhett Sr., "Father of Secession." James Legare built the house around 1833 and later sold it to Rhett, who lived here with a portion of his exceptionally large family (15 children from 2 wives). In 1863 Rhett sold it to future Confederate Treasury Secretary George Alfred Trenholm, who in 1866 sold it to partner Theodore D. Wagner. Both Trenholm and Wagner were involved in the Confederacy's most significant blockade-running company. The interior of the house has a gracious feel to it, in part, due to projecting polygonal bays on either side. Note the large garden that surrounds it in this early-twentieth-century photograph.

HOLY COMMUNION EPISCOPAL CHURCH. Located at 218 Ashley Avenue, the church has a long tradition of being the most liturgical of the Lowcountry's Episcopal churches. The building was initially constructed in 1855, but it has been expanded twice, including the installation of a lovely hammer-beam ceiling in 1871. Dr. Anthony Toomer Porter was rector of the church for many years and is responsible for its adherence to Anglican tradition. Reverend Porter also founded the Holy Communion Church Institute on the grounds of the former Federal Arsenal a block away, a school now known as Porter-Gaud.

LUCAS RESIDENCE. A dynasty of rice planters, and more importantly, rice millers, is associated with this handsome house located at what was once the end of Calhoun Street, number 286. Jonathan Lucas Jr. built this house, once surrounded by a large garden laid out by an English architect in the early nineteenth century. The builder's father, Jonathan Lucas Sr., came to Charleston after the Revolution and built the first water-powered rice mills in the country on the Santee River, north of Charleston. This development further encouraged rice culture in the Lowcountry, making it the pre-eminent source of wealth in the lower portion of the state. The house was later sold to the City, and the garden was destroyed to build a hospital. The residence was named the Riverside Infirmary and served private patients. At the time, the marshes of the Ashley River were within a few hundred yards of the house. Later the home served as the R.A. Kinloch Home for Nurses.

EPISCOPAL CATHEDRAL OF ST. LUKE AND ST. PAUL. At the turn of the century, the church was simply known as St. Paul's Radcliffeborough. As the city of Charleston grew above Boundary (Calhoun) Street, Episcopalians found it inconvenient to travel all the way to St. Michael's or St. Philip's from the Neck. Other reasons, including lack of space at existing churches and the preference for a recently dismissed priest from St. Philip's, may have contributed to the organization of the new congregation. St Luke and St. Paul's was built between 1811 and 1816 and is the largest Episcopal church in the city. Because actual costs far exceeded the original estimates for construction, the planned steeple was never completed. The truncated tower was decorated in a Regency Gothic style. Standing on Coming Street, the church has been a familiar landmark to generations of Charlestonians and the city's visitors.

INTERIOR OF 172 RUTLEDGE. In the early nineteenth century, the area above Boundary (now Calhoun) Street was a popular location for the wealthy to construct suburban villas as a refuge from the heat, disease, and congestion of the lower city. This home at 172 Rutledge Avenue was built during that era, likely around 1820. George Alfred Trenholm, a shipping magnate, owner of the most successful blockade-running firm, and secretary of the Confederate treasury, owned the home for many years. Trenholm later sold it to Charles Otto Witte, an export-import merchant and founder of the People's Bank. He and his Charleston bride, Charlotte Sophia Reeves, had the six most lovely, accomplished, and renowned daughters to ever grace the city: Carlotta, Fay, Belle, Laura, Alice, and Beatrice. The house was later sold to Miss Mary Vadrine McBee in 1908, who began, appropriately enough, a school for girls called Ashley Hall. Among its more famous alumna are Barbara Bush and Kate Jackson.

128

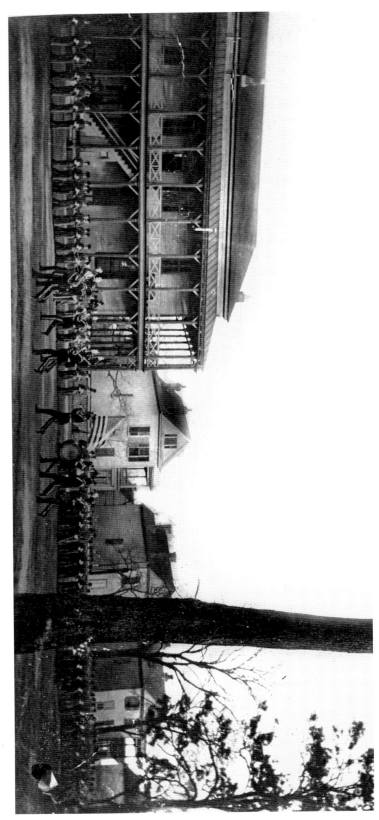

PORTER MILITARY ACADEMY. The troops shown here, students at one of Charleston's most prestigious educational institutions, were a familiar site in downtown Charleston for more than 90 years. The Reverend Anthony Toomer Porter founded the school, originally known as Holy Communion Church Institute, from his deep conviction that the South needed a school for children made destitute by the Civil War.

These photographs were taken in the 1890s when the founder, Reverend Porter, was still in charge. Despite the priest's gentle nature, he ruled with a firm hand. In 1895 a mini-rebellion by some students prompted severe action by Porter. A few cadets strongly criticized him and he asked them to apologize for the incident. One refused, and Porter ordered two sentinels to march the cadet out of the gate with fixed bayonets.

In 1963 Porter Military Academy merged with two other private educational institutions in Charleston to become Porter–Gaud School, which is coeducational. The school's campus is now located across the Ashley River from peninsular Charleston.

CHARLESTON'S ORPHAN HOUSE. This was not the orphanage of Oliver Twist; the city lavished its love and wealth on the house and its occupants. Most visitors were taken to see it at some point during their stay, and usually they came away awed. One British writer said it was "by far the most imposing edifice in the city," while a German nobleman noted "the very nourishing diet, and a truly maternal care, preserve the children healthy."

The building was constructed in two different eras. Thomas Bennett Sr. built the core between 1792 and 1794. It was a simple, four-story, brick structure. In 1853 architects E.C. Jones and Francis D. Lee presented plans to the orphan commission for an "enlargement and improvement of the house." They refashioned the building in the Italianate style, adding an entire floor, two wings, an addition in the rear, and restyled the cupola. A wooden statue of Charity crowned the building, which was 146 feet tall. Well-manicured grounds surrounded it, and Gabriel Manigault's Orphan House Chapel was in the rear. On the building's dedication, a local Episcopal priest, the Reverend C.C. Pinckney, set the tone for how his fellow citizens viewed the institution: "Greece and Rome erected temples and palaces which moderns have never rivalled. . . . Public buildings adorned [their] cities of colossal dimensions and lavish expenditure. . . . But the antiquary can point out among their architectural trophies, no asylum for the poor, the stranger, the widow, and the orphan. . . . It is our boast that temples of humanity adorn our cities in full proportion to their population and wealth."

The house's graduates provided the city with some of her most notable citizens, such as Christopher Memminger, Confederate secretary of the treasury and founder of the city's public school system, and Andrew Buist Murray, who left more than a million dollars to the City when he died. A traveler in the nineteenth century noted that many of the boys became naval officers after they left the home.

The aftermath of the war changed the city's economic circumstances, but Charlestonians still contributed what they could to the orphan children. By the middle of the twentieth century, attitudes had changed regarding the care and education of orphans. Large institutions like the Orphan House became antiquated relics. In the early 1950s, plans were made to move the children to a new facility in North Charleston.

ORPHAN HOUSE CHAPEL. Gabriel Manigault is credited with the design of a number of very important structures in the city. He designed no public building more elegant than this one, the Orphan House Chapel. The interior of the church had two paintings, including one of Christ blessing the children, and a Tiffany window given to the orphanage by its former resident, Andrew B. Murray. The window shows Christ holding a young child and says, "And he took them up in his arms, laid his hands upon them, and blessed them."

After the commissioners settled on a new location for the Orphan House, the old property was sold to Sears and Roebuck, which began demolition of the structures. Public opinion was split on the subject. Many citizens wanted a modern department store downtown though they hated to see the old buildings torn down. Others were completely opposed to the demolition. The Society for the Preservation of Old Dwellings received a guarantee from Sears that it would save the chapel.

The destruction of the Orphan House began in 1952. In February the demolition crews, finding that the statue of Charity and the great bell in the cupola were connected, attached steel cables to both and pulled them down. As they fell through the building, Charity broke in half, and the bell crashed to the ground with a loud thud. Shortly afterwards, workers began to pour the concrete foundations of the store that was "designed to conform to Charleston architectural tradition" and would be "one of the South's most modern and complete department stores."

Despite the store's promises, the chapel did not survive either. Sears complained that the site had insufficient parking. Locals stuck to their guns and argued that the chapel must be saved. They awoke in June of 1953 to find demolition crews at work taking the building down. A corporate spokesman said the chapel did not fit within the company's plans.

LOWER INCOME HOUSING. These unique photographs show a group of homes in the vicinity of the Medical University. Torn down in one of the city's few flirtations with slum clearance, they offer a picture of how "the other half lived" in the earlier half of the twentieth century.

BIRD'S-EYE VIEW OF THE WEST SIDE. This photograph also illustrates the living conditions of an area around the Medical University.

CHARLESTON NECK

The area above the original boundary line of Charleston was historically called "The Neck." This designation moved gradually northward as the city grew from its walled origins. Early city directories referred to anything above Boundary (Calhoun) Street as being "The Neck." Generally, the city's residents used the term to describe Charleston's less developed areas. For the purpose

of this book, the term is applied to the section above Line Street northward to the Naval Base.

Like the city's east and west sides, this area was quite diverse in the nineteenth century. Sizable truck farms, phosphate mills, and industrial establishments existed in the vicinity of suburban retreats and modest homes. In 1849 the City of Charleston annexed all land south of Mount

Pleasant Street, the last such move until the 1960s. Right after that annexation organizers laid out a number of cemeteries just north of the city limits for Charleston's varied religious and ethnic population. Later, the neighborhood was the site of a "world's fair" and is where the Navy established one of its largest bases.

ENTRANCE TO SANS SOUCI. In Charleston, as congestion increased, livability declined. Wealthier citizens purchased farms on the peninsula's "neck" (so-called because of narrowness of the land above the original city) to escape the heat, disease, and tumult. The estates were organized in a manner similar to like establishments in England. George Marshall owned this home from 1754 to 1767. The estate acquired the name Sans Souci around 1800. Some sources refer to it as the "Devereaux House." Though it was considerably damaged in Hurricane Hugo, a portion of the old house remains and is located at 203 Sans Souci Street.

COLORED INDUSTRIAL SCHOOL FOR ORPHANS. The orphanage operated the Colored Industrial School for Orphans, although the City gave an annual, token appropriation for the operation of the orphanage, reformatory, and the school. In an era when educators like Booker T. Washington molded racial policies, this institution represented mainstream thought. Reverend Jenkins in his report to the City in 1910 stated that the purpose of the school was "to train the father-less and mother-less children to become honest and industrious, prepared to fill any position in life as a servant. We train their minds to think and their hands to work."

COTTON PALACE. The South Carolina and West Indian Exposition in 1901–1902 was the culmination of years of efforts by the more progressive members of the city's business community. Beginning after the earthquake in 1886, the community sponsored a "Gala Week" to show that the city had recovered from the disaster and that business was thriving. Further efforts on the part of business interests brought conventions to the city, such as the Confederate Reunion in 1899 and the National Education Association in 1901.

A letter to the *News & Courier* proposed the initial idea of an exposition in 1899, pointing out that while many Southern cities had recovered from the effects of the Civil War, Charleston had lagged significantly despite many natural economic and geographic advantages. A "world's fair" would highlight the potential of the city and state and inaugurate a period of economic prosperity and growth of industry.

Efforts to bring about the event moved rapidly, and an architect was retained to construct a number of buildings for the fair, modeling them on the influential Chicago Columbian Exposition in 1893. The organizers retained Bradford Lee Gilbert, a New York architect, to design what became known as the "Ivory City" due to its use of ivory-tinted paint for the buildings. Mr. Gilbert described the result as having "a typical Southern character and motif" in a blend of the architecture of the "Colonial South and Ancient Spain" that "was fascinating beyond description." The builders used more than 2,500,000 square feet of lumber as well as 60 tons of nails, while painting more than 20 acres of surface area.

A handbook for the fair described the Cotton Palace as being "the most imposing building on the grounds, contained 600,000 feet of lumber. It was 320 feet long. The heart, or central part of the building, was 160 feet square, and the wings were 98 feet wide. The distance from the floor to the top of the dome was 185 feet." In the foreground of this photo are the Sunken Gardens; Anton Fiehe, the gardener of the famous Plant Railways in Florida, designed the landscape.

SOUTH CAROLINA BUILDING. The ornate structure was also referred to as the Palace of Agriculture. The guidebook stated, "In this structure are gathered the exhibits of various counties of the State. . . . Besides the great staples, cotton, rice, and lumber, there is an unnumbered list comprised in the word 'truck.' A study of these and the other exhibits reveals to some extent the vast resources of the State. The building is 400 feet long and 140 feet wide. In an annex to the rear are gathered exhibits of other States and Territories."

THE ORIGINAL NEGRO STATUARY. Initially planned for the front of the Negro Department Building, the statuary was moved because African Americans found the depiction offensive, so organizers moved it to a position in front of the Forestry and Mines Building, where it is shown here.

FINE ARTS GALLERY. More substantial than most of the other exposition buildings, the Fine Arts Gallery was also one of the most elaborate structures on the grounds. Inside was a large showing of the works of modern artists including Thomas Eakins, Childe Hassam, Winslow Homer, John Singer Sargent, and sculptors Frederic Remington, Augustus St. Gaudens, and Daniel Chester French. Local artists contributed extensively to the exhibition, and a section was reserved for historic artists including Thomas Sully, Gilbert Stuart, and Charleston miniaturist Charles Fraser.

THE COLONNADE. This scenic walk connected the Palace of Agriculture with the Cotton Palace.

THE PALACE OF AGRICULTURE AT NIGHT. Rows of incandescent bulbs lit the building's exterior lines, as well as the fountains and the Sunken Gardens. Charleston Consolidated Railway, Gas and Electric Company operated a separate power plant to serve the exposition's needs.

SUNKEN GARDENS. This is a view of the Sunken Gardens from the portico of the Cotton Palace looking toward the Auditorium. President Theodore Roosevelt addressed the public there on his visit to the exposition in 1902. The Auditorium seated 4,000.

HAMPTON PARK. Despite the great intentions and grand dreams of fair organizers, the exposition was a financial failure with the distinction of being the first world's fair to go into receivership. Significant appropriations by the City of Charleston and the State of South Carolina, along with support from several railways, were insufficient to sustain the exposition. Federal support was initially not forthcoming because of a rumor that the fair would not be on the scale of others at Philadelphia, Chicago, and Buffalo. A later grant of $160,000 proved to be inadequate. Subsequent action on the part of creditors, while the fair still operated, caused embarrassment for sponsors and bad publicity for the event.

Regardless, the exposition resulted in a number of positive improvements to the city. Two separate companies opened a cigar factory and an oyster-canning facility in Charleston, and a major fruit importer designated the city as its chief port in the United States. Sadly, construction methods forced the City to demolish all of the buildings at the exposition's conclusion, with the exception of an old plantation house used as the Women's Building. Perhaps the most lasting monument to Charleston's international fair was the establishment of Hampton Park afterwards. Seen here is the park's bandstand, remodeled for use in the park after the end of the fair.

MAGNOLIA CEMETERY. This is a nineteenth-century photograph of Charleston's Magnolia Cemetery. From the moment of settlement on the peninsula in 1680 until 1850, the majority of the city's inhabitants were buried in the city's churchyards and a couple of public grounds. The city leaders realized that this situation, if allowed to continue, would result in the ruin of the city's groundwater (its chief water source) and the health of its residents. A group of public-spirited men, who desired to establish a "rural cemetery" like those outside of Boston, Philadelphia, and New York, purchased a tract of land on the city's upper peninsula called Magnolia Umbra Plantation.

Its organizers laid out Magnolia in the romantic style favored during that era, with winding walks, reservoir pools, and large-scale planting of trees. It opened in 1850 with great ceremony; William Gilmore Simms gave the dedicatory ode while Charles Fraser, esteemed attorney and artist, delivered the address. Immediately the cemetery became a popular gathering place for the public. Local families took Sunday afternoon picnic trips to Magnolia, which was at the end of the streetcar line. The cemetery's spiritual significance increased with the interment of Confederate dead both during and after the Civil War.

Shown here is the grave of the Jones family in one of the decorative circles that composed a part of the original plan.

OPPOSITE PAGE: THE NAVAL YARD. The establishment of the Naval Yard at Charleston in 1901 was essentially the beginning of the city's modern era. The Yard and Naval Station provided employment for tens of thousands of residents during its history, ending a long period of economic stagnation. During World War II the Yard employed more than 25,000 civilians, who produced one new ship each week. Other defense installations followed after the war's end, including an air base and a naval weapons station, leading a wag to joke in Washington that if one more base were placed in Charleston, the whole city would sink into the rivers that surround it.

The first step in the development of the shipyard was the construction of a dry dock, shown in this photograph. Built between 1902 and 1908 at a cost of $7,250,000, the dock was 575 feet in length, 34 feet deep, and 112 feet wide at the top. Granite from Winnsboro, South Carolina, was used, totalling 10,000 dressed stones weighing an average of 2 tons each.

DISCOVER THOUSANDS OF LOCAL HISTORY BOOKS
FEATURING MILLIONS OF VINTAGE IMAGES

Arcadia Publishing, the leading local history publisher in the United States, is committed to making history accessible and meaningful through publishing books that celebrate and preserve the heritage of America's people and places.

Find more books like this at
www.arcadiapublishing.com

Search for your hometown history, your old stomping grounds, and even your favorite sports team.

Consistent with our mission to preserve history on a local level, this book was printed in South Carolina on American-made paper and manufactured entirely in the United States. Products carrying the accredited Forest Stewardship Council (FSC) label are printed on 100 percent FSC-certified paper.

MADE IN THE
USA